CW01011254

the mays 15

the mays 15

Guest edited by

Sean O'Brien & Colm Tóibín

Varsity Publications Ltd

First published 2007 by Varsity Publications Ltd
in association with Oxford Student Publications Ltd

Original concept by Peter Ho Davies, Adrian Woolfson, Ron Dimant

ISBN number 978-0-902240-43-8

A CIP catalogue record of this book is available from the British Library.

Varsity Publications Ltd
11-12 Trumpington Street
Cambridge CB2 1QA

http://mays.varsity.co.uk

Poetry

Contents

Prose

Artwork

Mathilda
Beatrice Priest

Before the Wedding
Miriam Arkush

Self Portrait
Naomi Grant

View From Train, Kerala
Marina Bradbury

Thanks
to our college sponsors...

Cambridge

Trinity, Jesus, Fitzwilliam, Emmanuel, King's, St Catharine's, St John's, Gonville and Caius, Magdalene, Newnham, Pembroke, Lucy Cavendish

Oxford

St John's, Christ Church, All Souls, St Hugh's, New College

and also to...

The Board of Directors and Editorial Team at *Varsity* and *Cherwell*, Didi Kuo, Alexander Oshmyansky, Pat Dalby, and everyone who submitted work

Poetry

Foreword
by Sean O'Brien

Even using such a relatively large sample as the several hundred poems submitted for this year's Mays anthology, it would be unwise to predict the emergent methods and preoccupations of young poets with any great confidence. What can be said is that the most interesting of the submissions are clearly the work of writers committed to the task of learning to write poetry, rather than simply passing through on the way to more permanent preoccupations.

There is also encouragement to be drawn from the fact that the couple of handfuls of poems that made the cut here are the work of writers who see life beyond the anecdote. A distinguished older poet recently commented, after reading his way through the poetry in some leading publications, that he'd encountered quite a few interesting anecdotes but very few properly developed poems. Anyone who's been paying attention to poetry in recent years will acknowledge that this was more than the curmudgeonly impatience of an elder of the tribe faced with the inclination of the young to do as they please rather than as he advises. There is, quite simply, far too much amiable, underpowered material in print from poets of all generations. Innumerable bits of melancholy / wry / affectionate / resentful autobiography are put through Granny's mangle in the outhouse (itself a not-infrequent subject) as though going through the motions could guarantee the resonance of the (not entirely) finished product.

The innocently conventional work of any period is of course likely to be bad: the degenerate, low-wattage realism I'm trying to evoke is simply our dose of the stuff. It's heartening to find poets looking trying to work in different ways. It would be fair to say, and it's hardly surprising, that the poems included here are honoured for the richness of their promise rather than the completeness of their achievement. What is most encouraging is their urgent imaginative ambition.

The exultant, at times rhapsodic detail of Benjamin's Morris's extended 'Sonata in Orange', a homage to Elizabeth Bishop, is the most obvious example. Neil Singh's 'On His Feet', at first sight a more familiar piece of work, about a Celtic supporter apparently dying from drink in hospital, offers an unhurried, compassionate attention to its material, enabling the poem to move beyond documentary to a satisfying sense of idiosyncrasy. Another lost soul figures in Rachel Piercey's 'The Woman in the Park', a clever, exact description of someone taking off a pair of lace gloves to feed the pigeons and then forgetting why. A comparable effort to dramatize anticipation as it finds itself deserted by events emerges in Emma Hoare's 'Cherry Blossom Poem', which follows the northward march of the blossoms across the islands of Japan.

The influence of Paul Muldoon, very important for older generations of poets, can be traced in the ingeniously sustained rhyming of Adam Crothers' 'Kid', as perhaps can the more abrasive soundscape of Simon Armitage, though neither presence suffocates this poem of comic exasperation. With Marcelle Olivier's 'wrong before: her healing' an intense realism of detail is used to estranging effect, while the packed stanzas of Muireann Maguire's 'Moscow Metro' sustain both objectivity and passion in her treatment of lost love: 'and I have nothing left of you, / not a token, not a word of a lie...' Aptly, the sometimes eerie relationship between art and life is explored in Meirion Jordan's 'The death and burial of Cock Robin', which is narrated by a taxidermist: 'twisting the skeletons of linnets / from wire by half an inch of tallow, / I am there again, nocking the sparrow's bow.' The marriage of attention and surprise in that closing image is the kind of thing the reader is always hoping for. If a poet can manage it once she might meet the challenge again. There are certainly grounds for optimism here.

Sean O'Brien was born in London in 1952. He is best known for his collections of poetry – The Indoor Park *(1983)*, The Frighteners *(1987)*, HMS Glasshouse *(1991)*, Ghost Train *(1995)*, Downriver *(2001), and his selected verse,* Cousin Coat *(2002). His verse translation of Dante's* Inferno *was published in 2006 and a new collection,* Manifest, *this year. Sean has also written extensively for stage, radio and television, and edited the acclaimed anthology* The Firebox: Poetry in Britain and Ireland after 1945 *(1998). He is now the Professor of Creative Writing at Newcastle University.*

Moscow Metro

by Muireann Maguire

five young men hang merrily from the rails
in crumpled jackets, swigging cups of vodka;
a young woman with sculpted purple nails
shuts her eyes, smiling, more serene
than the insane reflection cast behind her
nodding like a hanged man in the glass;
as the carriage tilts two lovers press
inches closer, teasing out a theme
practised as the journey, not yet old;
her body is a pillar in the wilderness
he touches her hair as if it were gold.

and I have nothing left of you
not a token, not a word of a lie,
not a needle to thread my dreams
through tunnels in the dark, when the train
changes pace, rattling, rocking the lovers
like dummies together, slowing down
-a woman slowly opens glazing eyes-
shakes us suddenly like a row of dolls
-the station lights scrape over our faces-
and pulls out, rolling in the dark
towards colder and less familiar places.

Head of an athlete in an Ionian shipwreck

by Meirion Jordan

Like two lovers laughing we surface
from the sea's kiss: my hand a stethoscope,
I can still hear it crashing in the cave
of your chest, the waves on Kassos.
Far down the sea tugs at us still,
the lobed seaweed and the lolling squid
begging us back, down into the blue dark,
our masks gasping into us as we
go diving on the wreck, its hull yawed up,
our hands divining cargoes of wrought marble,
silt. And still that youth looks out
from windowless sand, his eyes serene and blank:
down there his smile is white as alum,
inviting as a blue infinity of fish. Already
I can feel my body tilting to him like a level, already
we are going down again and perfectly still
we fly into the blue silence like stones.

The death and burial of Cock Robin

(Walter Potter, taxidermist, 1835-1918)

by Meirion Jordan

But when I think of it, the days
among copse and hedgerow
wringing the necks of birds
to leave the skin intact, the nights
in the deserted stable loft
twisting the skeletons of linnets
from wire by half an inch of tallow,
I am there again, nocking the sparrow's bow,
my fingers blotched with mercury. Then
it was a wonder, all the birds
under one canopy and fame
followed me at last to this museum,
my own house. But that half inch
is still my separation from the dark,
from the glass tears of birds
I fletched in parodies of flight.
At night I hear their psalms,
the shovel rattling on earth
and further off, the white owl's eyes
bulging like moons over a narrow grave.

Sonata in Orange

(for Elizabeth Bishop)

by Benjamin Morris

This morning
I peeled the last clementine,

its brazen skin
falling softly to the floor

as though
it were auditioning for gravity.

I slipped
the fat crescents against my cheek,

letting one sac spray
at a time, the juice running thin

and cold and clear
between my teeth. Early autumn

and I've thrown
the day away to travel:

three o'clock
and through the train window

the sun slides
its knife across my chest;

thick shadows
of house and tomb give way

to fields whose
curves and soft undulations

must have been
what the old painters were looking for,

not what was there
but what we wanted to see—

crops raked
and combed by sunlight, creamy birds

dripping from
the clouds. There's a word in my head

I can't seem
to get out: *panoply*. And another:

vestments. And
another, and another after that, a word

for each
of these folds in the earth, each

of these sheep
salting the plains, words into infinity,

into everywhere,
into all the coughs and rustlings

of all
the other travelers on this train,

into myself,
into nowhere at all. Into the clouds,

placid, massive
ice floes sailing the silent sky.

Into colours
not yet seen, into orange, a colour

caught between
two lives, spun across the sound

of one belief
forming. No one knew where we were

an hour ago,
gliding to the top of the world

where strange winds
tousled the loose dirt and snow

into a kind of
lunar vegetation, spreading into evening

with a tenderness
received because we could not

ask for it.
Yet there the eye had no house

large enough
anymore to chamber such rich texture.

It seemed too
as though part of the earth

had dropped away
and taken all the colour with it,

save for that
we had smuggled with us on the train.

Oh Elizabeth,
you saw sun behind a hill

rim the trees
into blurred and smoky shadows,

you know
the fear of the indistinct

and its awful
and graceful beginnings—where

have you gone,
and why have you left us, alone,

on a train,
avoiding our destination? Night, now,

and the air
empties. They say the cosmos

kills a body
not because of what it does, but because

of what it fails
to do: pressurize the blood, permit the cells

their slow leavings
and unleavings. How swiftly the mind

wraps itself
around this fact, draws near

to the warmth
given off by an idea as violet and

unknowable
as gravity, as the body next to me,

a body reading,
a mind wrapped in the fictions

of its own
fashioning. Beneath us the waters

roll and swallow
in the moonlight as though made

of molten silver,
in the long languor of things

not having names
nor needing them. Wind stirring the reeds,

a first sound
rippling over the lake, still sounding.

They may not
have bought it but he sure sold it

to them—
the language comes whirling in

on skates,
turning and twisting as if wanting

to recall
a place it had long forgotten,

a place with
clementines and wine, and words

and gestures
ripe for falling into memory's basket,

thatched with stars
whose light still flirts with time.

Soon we will
take down the old patterns from the shelf,

dust them
for the coming evening, retire

to the sunroom
while the birds dream their slim nests

together.
Soon this remembrance too

will be held
to the light like a gem.

We all want
to die near the river: mirror, mirror

on the glass,
enough of the future, tell me my past.

Shore and rock, froth
and foam, tell me where my heart will roam.

On His Feet

by Neil Singh

It is better to die on your feet than live on your knees.
José Martí

I

There are the usual clues:
puncture wounds snaking
up his limbs; breadcrumbs
leading to a tender liver.
The right striking,
the left pressed flat,
my middle fingers tap his abdomen
as if knocking a barrel, listening
for the plimsoll line, that point
where air becomes wine.

I was told to look
for signs in his eyes.
His square, lacquered pupils
are bordered by an off-white frame,
but it's the sallow Polaroid
he fingers edgily
that gives the game away.

II

He's on his feet again,
shuffling outside for a breather,
sporting his matching strip. The nurses tut
as he stages another great

escape. They reckon he gangs
up with old pals to share a joke
or more; subtle and fleeting
as two hands at midnight.
Once, I clocked him
sneaking a cheeky fag,
watching his wasted fingers kick
the ash tumbling, curling
to concrete.

III

I sit at the foot of his bed, watching him
treat his battered slippers; looping the tape
taut as laces, lovingly darning the torn sole.
They offered him a substitute pair
but he'll hold on
to these all through the Autumn,
even when sore cracks shoot
up his heels.

IV

His ribbed, black socks flop
thickly around his ankles, and were noted thus:
"Mr. McManus is off his food again".
But still, the doctors gloss over something
Tom would never miss:
the way his fusty knee-highs
complement his light green gown.

These are the colours of Glasgow
away from home.

Raleigh

by Rachel Piercey

His mother's friend had been ashed
at the stake, into little cinder leaf pieces.
You could birth a calf in the time it took,
or launch a ship, or learn to love a girl
with red hair and skin like the innards
of fruit, or new food, or the tips of waves.
She smiled like sighting land, America
of lakes and mountains, lapped and framed
and unmapped, unmanned, vast and stormed,
with a moat of ocean. Her words were
burning trees on a wet night, respite for a
traveller who had spanned seas, tall and frozen,
but who couldn't let his love get cold feet.
She favoured such acts of devotion.

The Woman in the Park

by Rachel Piercey

The woman in the park wears lace gloves.
They are unfit for feeding pigeons,
so when she does, she slips them off as if
she were undressing for a lover.

The wrists first; the tiny iris buttons
winking and dipping under her fingers.
Soon they are on show, growing like young trees,
or spilt cream, a curiously waxing moon.

Then, the palms, a skirt eased off the hips.
The blue rivulets, the swell below the thumbs,
are revealed slowly, in quarter inches.
The arches of the fingers start to show.

She gathers round herself, leans in to see
her peeled hands, as if for the first time,
and they wriggle like toes, like a child.
They could carry out so many things.

Sometimes she forgets to feed the birds,
and often they just fly away.

wrong before: her healing

by Marcelle Olivier

the ruby is a recent strain.
her lips have turned, and they flush
like street-signs in headlights. the colour
is deep and provocative,
as if she were thirteen again.
then with small and cramping breasts
that streaked through her school-shirt:
a pair of stones that wore down the cotton
like metal at miners' fingers;
now again they shine translucent in the dark, pointing
at the seams gleaming underground.

the dusty remains of her lashes
turn men on. their stares are heavy,
sniffer dogs circling her pupils, excited
by the water humming its tune inside,
swishing with each sway of an iris
as she tries to avoid their gaze.
they clearly love the smell of her face, and close in
at the tills or in lifts; she sees their tongues
flick out from between their lips, wishing for a taste
of the fall-out from a brittle blink.

the last week has been difficult on her waist, too.
it has blossomed into something sleek
and subtle, and unmeant flirts just tumble from her hips
when she moves. the teenage dip in her stomach
is back: when she could wear anything – baggy
colours, tight whites, navy high school dresses
bothered by wide belts and superfluous pleats –

Mathilda
Beatrice Priest

Before the Wedding
Miriam Arkush

Self Portrait
Naomi Grant

View From Train, Kerala

Marina Bradbury

and it would melt into the knob of unused womb
riding above the pelvis like a carefully weighted balance.
like her lips, her bellybutton reflects flames, turning visible.

in the hospital there is respite. she is mostly ignored
by nurses who bring weak ginger teas
and are violent with her sheets; they know
she has been cursed with life and they keep her
so unseen. but sometimes the specialists still
say she is lucky, for few bear it out
so beautifully: her paled skin is clear, her hair
is soft. she improves a bit every day.
the young doctors fall in love over
needles caressing her veins, and ask questions
about her future. as if she was thirteen.

Cherry Blossom Poem

by Emma Hoare

Sakura
Sakura!
The news smiles its report
As the Cherry Blossom Front
Marches up Japan.

Every island, every city, every park:
Buds nose and fatten dumbly
Then a silent, slow night snow,
And the frill-lipped papers crush out, kicking skirts-
An incoherence of blossoms

Crowding the sky, chattering
With crimped, shivering edges
Spreading out, and back, and wide-
Three days, maybe seven, or five, and
The branches sag,
A palliasse of ripen scent.

Behind the city
Hills explode
Pink, flesh, cream, white.
Cherry blossom jelly, sweets and ice.

And the moon is an inflamed eye
Pollen dusted, swollen. Blind
All night, as incense breathes from the
Ghost petals, luminous in the dark,
Bushels of curving smiles, a moan, a word,
A floating point.

They rub together, staticky
Drifts of cloud over taxis, dark streets.
Then unlatching
Like a breakdown, pointlessness- a poem-
Strange rain.
No release; just baring branches and
Pink slick, drunk dregs.
Perfume drowning the soil.

Kid

by Adam Crothers

She threw you out to wander in mudfields guttered
by four-by-fours, in the attire of a goatherd
as you thought it, all coarse hair and sackcloth gathered

from bombsites. Eating insects and birds. You muttered
to the goat's-cheese moon of feeling stepped on, murdered,
of missing milk and butter and being mothered,

as if hooves like yours couldn't be clasped together,
or as if butting your stump-horned head into a puddle mattered.

Prose

Students
by Colm Tóibín

I am, therefore I think, the philosopher said, and that seems reasonable, just as the idea that I itch therefore I scratch cannot be argued with. A novel is a thousand lies, and a longer novel maybe two thousand. What is strange about reading is that it is silent and solitary, yet if you were told that the novel you are reading existed only in this one copy and was only to be read by you at this one sitting, the experience of reading would seem immediately more insubstantial and oddly worthless. Why is this?

I am, therefore I think, this seems hardly worth mentioning, because you do not know what I am thinking. Science cannot help us, despite the many superior minds which have applied themselves to the matter. Yet in fiction, we can tell what someone is thinking, and we can start believing it, which makes fiction so subversive and oddly satisfying. It is the only time when both the writer and reader can be God, which must be, if we are properly human at all, our main ambition for ourselves during our time on the earth.

This is one of the modes of fiction which we take for granted: the words will register the mind at work. In Eric Morgan's 'Wild and Tame' and Francesca Whitlum-Cooper's 'Last Words', for example, we have third person intimate - the sensuous mind, the business of remembering, reflecting and noticing captured as though in real time. Time is slowed down, moved swiftly forward, then subtly back, the world is made flesh by the use of detail after detail. What happens depends on what is noticed. Sophie and Laura, by allowing the reader to see the world through their eyes, become the reader, or the reader becomes them. They both know how easily the past can come back, despite the pressing business of the present. The both become aware that the drama of noticing the world, the drama of being in the world, is to be disrupted and sharpened, almost shaped, by memory.

My editor in New York, on having lunch with a rather fierce author, and expecting to be asked about sales figures and marketing plans, was asked instead: 'What do you think about form in American writing?' For most writers, this tiny brusque encounter would be enough. Henry James loved being told just half such a story, so he could make up the rest. A whole story was no use to him. But I needed to know the end. 'What did you say?' I asked. She replied: 'I said that American writers care so much about voice, that form hardly comes into the picture.'

All of us care about voice. A sentence begins as an accident and ends as a design. Begins in voice and ends in form. If the voice is missing, the form is redundant. Some writers are all voice; their aura is all over even the silent blank pages. If the phone rang, you would know from the timbre of the ringing tone that it was them. All of us play with this idea of asking the reader to notice the voice and then begin the seduction of the reader by lowering the voice, or trying to say something so true, or so incredible, or so funny that the reader ceases to notice the voice or time passing or the form or the idea that these are just marks on a page.

Thus the first person voice in Laura Hocking's 'Johnny', Benjamin Morris's 'The Rhythm of Black Lines' and Ryan Roark's 'The Center of the Universe' plays with us, invites us home, begins to whisper, becomes suddenly intimate with us. We do not notice form, and see no artistry. We hear, instead, a living voice. There are moments in these three stories when there is space left for the reader to say 'are you serious?' or 'go on' or 'what happened next?'. The voice, merely because of the tone which is held and wielded, seems to possess a face, a body, a history. Slowly, as the voice speaks, it reveals more than it states, we begin to know more about the personality behind the voice than the speaker does. Knowing more is a form of pleasure; knowing more is the most fun we will ever have with all our clothes on.

When in doubt, take your character to a public place. A party, a disco, a rave, an opening night in the theatre. Stop them watching themselves, having it all their way. Let the world notice them, ignore them, hurt them. See them as though from a distance. The reason God made public spaces was for us to live in fear of them. The controlled self with the pulse beating faster because someone is watching. Jane Austen did it all the time – establish the character in pure privacy, allow for much overnight reflection, and then pounce – have a dance, a dinner. In Claire Lowdon's 'The Amphibians' and Christopher Morley's 'The Changing Room' we realise that for a writer there is gold in a dressing room, a place where people take their clothes off and hang them up, where people are suddenly vulnerable but have to behave as though it is all normal. The drama comes from the idea of masking and unmasking in a public space; the conflict between the soft flesh and the hard tiles makes the reader hope that this is all happening to someone else.

The act of undressing in public can be slow, sly drama or fast, showy and fearless. Fiction has many mansions. One of them makes the reader feel that the rooms are real, the atmosphere oddly familiar, until the reader forgets everything, and follows the words as though they were Gospel. And then someone comes along to announce that the mansion is merely bricks and mortar, or is on fire so you had better run. Lawrence Sterne did this, so too James Joyce, Nabokov, Borges,

Beckett, Angela Carter, Donald Bartheleme. In Heather Mcrobie's 'Mostar Bridge, Summer 2005' and Simon Pitt's 'When Lunch Becomes Dinner', the game is up with fooling the reader with details, the job is to unfool the reader, or send the fool farther with footnotes. The job is to open the mansion to the public, demystify its grandeur, put in false doors and blind windows, make night day just because you decide, make the lady of the house cook for the cook, leaving out half of the ingredients and making the food all the more delicious for that. Eat.

These nine stories then prove, if we need proof, that there is no formula for fiction, which is itself a sort of formula. Our formula insists that science does not help us, and a paragraph of philosophy compared to a paragraph set in a changing room, or in bed, or in memory, seems oddly dry and pointless. We exist because we cannot help it, but it is far more interesting that when we itch, the scratching can be delicious. It is the job of the fiction writer to make both the itch and the scratch more real than marks on the page and more delicious than dinner.

Colm Tóibín was born in Enniscorthy, Co. Wexford in 1955. His most recent novels The Blackwater Lightship *(1999) and* The Master *(2004) were both shortlisted for the Man Booker Prize. He has published several works based on his extensive travels, including* Homage to Barcelona *(1990) and* The Sign of the Cross: Travels in Catholic Europe *(1994), and other non-fiction, most recently, a collection of essays* Love in a Dark Time: Gay Lives from Wilde to Almodovar *(2002). In 1999 he edited* The Penguin Book of Irish Fiction. *His latest work is a collection of short stories,* Mothers and Sons *(2006).*

Wild and Tame

by Eric Morgan

It had been a deliberate decision, not a lapse of judgment.

"The pig didn't escape by accident. I opened the gate. I wanted to set it free," said Sophie, with the thrilling pride of rebellion, laughing as we drove north.

When she was younger, her elementary school had kept a pet pig penned up in the yard.

We were driving up to Gravenhurst, where she was from and near where my parents owned a cottage.

"After lunch, all us kids would rush and take all our garbage, melon rinds, apple cores, sandwiches, you know, and throw it over the fence for the pig to eat. One boy in my grade, Stanley McCulloch, used to not eat his sandwich just so that he could feed it to the pig. The gross part was that his mom always packed him a ham and cheese sandwich. The pig's name was Stewart, but Stanley always called him Wilbert. He was a dumb kid. I think his mom drank when she was pregnant with him. Idiot. When you were throwing in your garbage you had to be careful."

"Why?" I asked, always the straight man.

We were driving north through the Holland Marsh with its stinky fecundity, wide and verdant, busy with early spring.

"Because the pig might bite off your fingers. Every year somewhere in Ontario at least one farmer gets eaten by his pigs."

I doubted that.

"It's true. Our teachers always told us so and it was always someone's cousin's uncle. The pigs, between slop feedings and mud rollings, come to the logical conclusion that either the farmer eats them or they eat the farmer. They're really smart and really vicious. Of course afterwards they're always destroyed, unless they escape."

The pig grew enormously fat, fat as a banker, until one day the principal decided that it was time to ship it away for slaughter.

Sophie and I drove on. She sat there in my plaid shirt, looking out the window, smiling.

"I found Stanley McCulloch weeping in the washrooms that day. When the line-up was too long at the girls, I'd go into the boys. I could tell he was there because he'd been spending so much time around Wilbert that he stunk like pig. Stanley was just crouched down in a stall, paralyzed with grief, so I grabbed him by the hand and I marched him outside to the pigpen. Wilbert was there, soaking up the sun, caked in cracked mud, grunting and snorting about. I grabbed Stanley's hand and together we opened the gate. Wilbert just waddled around in circles inside the pen, so I picked up a stick and jabbed him in the butt like we saw that matador poke a bull on the TV. He took off out of that gate and flew out of the schoolyard and galloped down the dusty road like something else, like a wild shadow. Stanley gave this happy scream as Wilbert sped off. He clapped his dirty little hands with idiotic glee. He loved it. Loved it!"

That was all before I met her, before she graduated from high school and moved to Toronto and before we met at the university.

"Of course it didn't do any good. Wilbert was hit by a car a little while later. They'd have caught him eventually any way."

We drove on and on.

I had not had childhood adventures like Sophie had, so I liked listening to hers. I had not gone down to the swimming hole, with its muddy mysterious water and swinging rope. There had been no swimming hole to go down to. I had not had a gang or schoolyard brawl. Sam

Morgenthaul, a kid who ate erasers, was the closest we ever came to having a pet pig at my school. I had never broken my leg or gotten dirty or gotten into trouble. When she spoke of her childhood, she described a landscape I had never seen.

As we drove north, we passed over the Severn River and the land became rocky with jolly, stubborn pines poking out of the shallow earth. Chubby clouds chuckled above, bemused by what was below, at least I thought so.

Both of my parents were lawyers in Toronto. They were brilliant and brittle and happy and weak and witty and safely celibate. Our cottage was on a little lake, plain and placid. My parents would don bug hats and big rubber boots and garden in the biting haze of mosquitoes, suffering for fun over the unprofitable, unyielding soil. They massacred dandelions with the lawnmower in a golden shower of damaged petals and they murdered anthills with hoes. Then when the job wasn't quite done, but they'd had enough, they went inside to read the Saturday papers. Once, after I had mowed the lawn, I found a slimy and smooth leopard frog, limping in circles, off balance with only one leg, a bloody stub, like a returning soldier might have. There wasn't anything to be done, though. I put the lawnmower away and let unforgiving nature take its course.

It was easy to be brave at that cottage. Jumping off the raft into the dark enveloping water in my underwear at sunset was brave. It was easy to be brave at that cottage because so much was forbidden and frightening.

We drove on, past a family nudist resort called Taboo, past a bouncing Baptist church that was right next to a naughty video store, past a sign that informed us with bureaucratic calm that a prison was nearby and we should not pick up hitchhikers.

"When prisoners escaped they would keep us in for recess. I don't know why. It's a minimum-security prison for white-collar criminals. What's the worst that could happen? Some crooked accountant bludgeons you with a ledger? It happened quite frequently because the place has about as much security as a kids' summer camp."

She was brightening as we drove closer to Gravenhurst where her parents ran a motor repair shop. Gravenhurst had motors. Gravenhurst had truckers, handymen, drycleaners, and tourist shops with goofy merchandise that no one who lived locally would be caught dead buying, except maybe as a gag gift. The town had one adulterous motel, three bank branches, four sullen grocers, seven doctors, fifty-two teachers of varying competence and one judge. The judge had four clerks and zero friends. How could it have been otherwise? The men had mustaches and the women had prayer groups.

But before we visited her parents, we had to go to my cottage to pick some furniture for our apartment back in the city.

As we drove, the clouds above lost their joy. The sky grew gray and then black and it began to rain heavily, big globs of water falling down.

"How much stuff did they say we could have?" she asked, staring out the window at the spreading countryside, soaking and soggy now with the angry rain.

"A sofa and a couple of chairs."

"We can't lift a couch."

"No, you're right. That's why my dad called Johnson to help us."

Johnson was the local man who was unsatisfactorily renovating our cottage over the winter. His progress was annoyingly sporadic and he missed the deadlines that he himself set. All smoke, no fire.

We reached the cottage and the van tumbled down a tree-hooped tunnel as we drove down the gravel driveway. Johnson was already there with one of his shifty buddies.

I got out of my van and they got out of theirs.

"Well, little mister, how are you?"

He choked my hand. His fingernails were chipped short. His fingers were swollen with tendons and the palms were coarse with work.

The rain flooded down very thick and warm. The soft gravel was studded with beer bottle caps like colorful, stunted mushrooms. Half of the cottage was painted white, the other half pealing blue.

Johnson's buddy stood beside him. He had a slow look about him and his far-off eyes were permanently staring into an uncertain distance.

Sophie came round from the other side of my van.

"Stanley McCulloch?" she exclaimed when she saw who Johnson's buddy was. "How are you?"

Stanley McCulloch dropped his vigil of faraway things and looked at Sophie, but without recognition. The four of us silently stood still under the splashing sky, all of us waiting for an answer. The trees sweated off the rain, their interlocking branches drip-dropping and heavy. The air was warm, wet and tense. It looked like the scene of a murder before the incident.

"Stanley, it's Sophie. How the hell are you?"

The speechless forest seemed to draw closer like a crowd around a fight. Johnson finally answered for him.

"He's fine. He's been helping me here about."

Stanley didn't say a word, but brought up a silly smile from somewhere inside like he was enjoying a joke none of us could hear.

"Well," said Sophie, plucking up control after the rebuff, "we've got some furniture to get going, so let's get going."

The men were slow to move. They went into the cottage and easily carried out the heavy sofa into the rain.

"No, no. That won't work. We'll get the chairs first."

They carted the sofa back into the cottage and we got

the chairs and put them quickly in our van. The rain came down and soaked everything.

"Okay, now get the couch."

They brought it out again, with a little more difficulty this time, groaning a little under their breaths. They tried to put the sofa in my van, but it wouldn't fit. Everyone was rushed, what with the rain, which began to drench the sofa in large pellets, pop, pop, pop. Ratatatat, shishboomba.

"Maybe if we'd put the couch in first," Johnson said, resentful and red from having to hold up the sofa for so long. He looked like he couldn't hold it much longer.

"No, no," Sophie said in a curt command. She climbed into the van and out of the rain and bent over to guide the sofa in. They tried again and someone fumbled and slipped and the sofa went down and heavily hit the ground and also crushed Johnson's foot.

Johnson yelled and his face flamed with pain, his thick fists clenching and unclenching as he gave me a wild stare. I stood there motionless, slim and slight. Sophie was bent over inside the van. Stanley had his idiot's greedy grin on his face as he looked down Sophie's shirt, dangling open. It was as if a cloud had eclipsed the sun or a spider had descended down on a silver thread. It was as if a great wind had blown open a gate and then blown the whole thing down. For a moment, there was menace. Then the moment passed.

"Try again," Sophie said, with a lightness as if nothing had happened.

They got the sofa in and we drove to see Sophie's parents.

I realized, in that moment, how close we were to the frontier of everything. The dark and the wild were always there. It was an incessant cold creeping, always quietly pushing, a rocky reclaiming. It wasn't life, it was death against which we were grappling.

We drove back to Toronto.

"Well, that furniture expedition was something else," I said with relief, cheerfully looking southward on the road.

In a quick twist Sophie turned in her seat and handed me down a look of squirming disgust. Then she turned back to face the window and the land, confident and carefree, saying, "It wasn't that stormy."

As we drove south, the land became dark until I couldn't see Sophie's silent face next to me in the van. I could only see her eyes in the dark, drawing in all the renegade rays of the dusk and reflecting them back in two solid circles. The shadows of the night made all forms foreign and unfamiliar. It was like driving into a new city.

Last Words

by Francesca Whitlum-Cooper

Laura sits in the front room of her North London terrace surrounded by History. Prints and lithographs of a bygone era covered the walls of this house long before such decoration became popular and Framed Historical Scenes were flying off the shelves in John Lewis and Peter Jones. Books line its walls, shelves burst at their seams – out of *interest* this is, out of intellect, study, not from any aesthetic preference. The office itself breathes age, from years of books and papers and the intelligent dust of accumulation: age is in its smell, its taste, the feel of the beaten leather and polished wood on the skin.

A magazine from the Sunday paper catches her eye, one of the newest additions to the room since 1999's splash-out on a new computer. Its cover: a man parading around his three-bedroom Ruislip semi in a Georgian aristocrat's frock coat, a freak show for the modern world. She faintly smiles, as those who live this side of the Holloway Road do at such a thing, ridiculous but somehow quaint in its absurdity. There is pity in the twitch which darts across her lips for this man in his powdered wig, devoted to something so distant. Somehow her life, encased in this house – itself encased with books and documents and references and the British Museum poster of the Magna Carta hanging in the downstairs toilet – isn't in her eyes the same homage to the ever-present yet unachievable past. Even the magazine, hanging precariously off the edge of the battered Hampstead Antiques leather sofa, is an addition to the history charted in her ledgers and databases. Her life encompasses her work, it *is* her work, her History – the "additions to": the additions to the sources in relation to the 1861 Bill on Education, the additions to the books on shelves and articles on the Internet, the additions to the respectable lives and marriages continuing under their own steam all around the world, with no particular need, support or interest other than companionship for that Welsh newsreader's beautifully read ten o'clock news and Saturday's trip to Sainsbury's.

In this antiquated atmosphere time passes unnoticed. On the hour, every hour, the clock in the hallway chimes its high, muted chime: the rest of the time its faint ticks unobtrusively permeate the house, an almost-silent presence in every corner. On occasion Jeffrey will come and go, the neat tap-tap of his highly polished accountant's shoes the only indication of presence moving into absence. Other things move too, in this seemingly static house. Over the years, smiles turn into flicks of the lips – grotesque if you study them too long – and finally into nothing more than acceptance. Somehow Time has moved her into the continent of middle-age, well and truly landlocked. Not hard, she supposes, when one's husband is a chartered accountant with a lifelong hatred of the sea, when 'for better, for worse' has meant that long weekends in the Peak District have slowly crept up on the heady seaside summers of youth. Oddly enough, she hasn't minded. There is something terribly comfortable in the easiness of acceptance, experience the age-old placater of the urge for Revolution.

And all the while she sits at her desk. Minutes, into hours, into days, and beyond: reading, scribbling, annotating, rereading. It is years since she stopped giving lectures, reasoning instead that further research is a much worthier and more efficient use of this infinite expanse of time. Because while there is her branch of History, the "additions to", there is also the other branch. The "might have beens": what might have happened if the peasants hadn't revolted, or if D-day had failed, or if any of the other endless possibilities that for some unknown reason had failed, had come into play. She learnt long ago that this branch of History is futile: exciting, maybe, but useless, and – she reminds herself with an optical flicker of disdain – an almost exclusively a male preoccupation. Her degree and subsequent career have taught her that for eight out of every ten "might have beens", there's a better solution, a better outcome: fewer deaths, fewer merciless regimes, fewer revolutions, fewer bodies lying in the streets, fewer lives meaninglessly wasted and/or destroyed. Additions are neater, easier on the soul, "more fulfilling" the old adage goes, more beneficial in the long run. And that is Laura's problem: the long run, the pandemic with the smiling face sweeping through lives and decisions everywhere. Laura has always lived for the long run, and that is why today, she has frozen.

It has come out of the blue: a big, bold, invasive line in her Inbox which has shattered the tranquillity of number 47 Highbury Gardens, and sent her flying into oblivion. She hasn't spoken to him in years, at least in the fifteen she has been married. His name comes out of the anonymous, Internet abyss like a dull pain, a blunt stab in the back of the throat. Colour flies to her face, russet against her white shirt: her throat is rusty, her breath is the sharp exhalation of smoke on cold mornings. Is it not enough that she has agreed to give her first lecture in seven years? Is it not enough that she is already sleepless, already suffering the paralysing palpitations of stage-fright at the most mundane hours of the day and night? And now, to hear from him, to have him there… *Nathaniel Waters*. Her lips form the words breathlessly. The lilting syllables alone transport her instantly back to the hazy, golden glow of university summers: cheap wine in warm fields, easy love in steamy cars. She cannot remember the last time the world was knocked off its axis. It scares her. The ticking of the clock is louder now, bouncing off the walls into her ears. The silence of her house is no longer tranquil, it is invasive, threatening. She can feel the air being sucked into this room, the weight of it surrounding her, crushing her lungs. A car pulls up outside. The familiar tap-tap of fifteen married years makes its way towards her up the path. Between the key hitting the latch and the twitch of its turn, there is a split second where time stops. She decides. Leaning on the table, she slowly begins – a swimmer on the bank who has not for years felt the icy coldness of the water as it threatens to overwhelm – to type her response.

Two weeks later, the Tube journey has been fine. The Northern line has been fine, has unobtrusively chugged its way into the heart of the capital. At every station new faces have thrust themselves forward to find a seat, only to stare at the crotch of the person standing in front of them as their bodies are numbed by the dull monotony of the motion. At Camden Town an extensively pierced young man stands up to give her his seat. She finds it ridiculous that she can seem this old. It is only when a second passenger offers his seat at King's Cross that she resigns herself to it. Gaggles of school girls, all non-existent skirts, blonde manes and makeup – more makeup on each fifteen year old face than she has ever owned – crowd together in convulsions of laughter and gossip. Laura stares: their confidence is magnetic, she is intoxicated and appalled – apparently there is nothing embarrassing about discussing last night's sex in a carriage so crowded you can hear the stranger next to you breathing. She is not sure whether she would not do so because she is embarrassed, or because she cannot remember precisely the last time she engaged with Jeffrey in their clumsy, married couplings. Their loud, look-at-me stance is effective. From the other side of the crowded carriage a group of boys stare, enveloped in dark hoods and trousers that hang from their scrawny bodies. Pure noise pumps from the headphones around their necks, and they talk in a language Laura cannot understand. The experience unnerves her. She is not a recluse, she adamantly tells herself, she is *not*: she goes out every weekend, she reads the papers, she knows all about the hoodie phenomenon, the rise of hip hop, and the alarming rate of teenage pregnancy, but somehow this carriage, with its pheromones and thudding baseline, is unutterably alien. She doesn't want to be old, she doesn't want to be the woman who stands on the wrong side of the escalator, or who loses her travel card in the gulf of her handbag, but suddenly today, she is. It hits her like a brick as she sits on the number 91 bus. After years of not caring, today, the one day in fifteen years in which she has *wanted* to look young, *wanted* to look beautiful, *wanted* to have elegant clothes and expensive taste, she realises that she is old. The course, grainy texture of the brick slides down her throat, grazing, asphyxiating, and settles, a dead weight in her stomach, the sharp corners pressing her gizzards. Amidst the clouds of brick dust, confusion and bus fumes, she sees her stop, and presses the bell.

Once inside King's, her world goes into fast-forward. The one function she has never properly mastered on the video at home now hurls her forward at an alarming pace. Her feet scrabble to keep up with the student taking her to her destination; they slip on the shiny floors; walls and people hurtle past in a blur of noise and colour and texture, scratchy wool, crunchy overcoat, faint wafts of exotic fragrance and stale cigarette smoke. Up endless flights of stairs, along corridors, through unmarked doors, she vaguely hopes someone will guide her back. More stairs, fluorescent lighting, she can feel the papers in her bag, the plastic handles of the bag itself steadily threatening to slip. Has she got everything?

She hopes to God she has. The lecture, her notes, the projector – will someone be there to work the projector? And all the while in the back of her mind, the thought that he is here, somewhere in this building, somewhere in this rat-run of corridors and passages, this labyrinth. She thinks she should have brought a ball of string to guide herself back – then self-chastisement: Stop it, she tells herself. She is sure that success, confidence and youthful beauty do not lie in pathetic witticisms based on classical myth.

And then – they are there. Travis or Tristan, the slightly grimy blonde Adonis leading her, complete with jeans so low slung they show a good six inches of underwear, and a hand-knitted Incan poncho, makes to go. She asks naively whether he'll be staying. No, he doesn't go to lectures. *Obviously*. As she stutters her thanks, she blinks into the bright light of the lecture room. She remembers it now, the lectern, the screen, thankfully a projector. She is early. There are two or three students scattered about the room, mostly leaning on their desks: it is difficult to tell if they are asleep, or, indeed, whether they will wake up when she begins. Something tightens in her throat. As she walks up to the stage, her court shoes make the same tap-tap as Jeffrey. How ironic, she thinks.

Twenty minutes later the room is filling up. She has not dared to look at her audience, instead busying herself with any activity which allows her to keep her eyes firmly lowered. Their lids seem to burn with the bright light and the noise of the voices. Her hands shake as she rearranges her papers, her slides. They are covered in a thin layer of moisture: touching the acetate leaves a sweaty fingerprint. She tries to rub them surreptitiously, but their hot clamminess sticks to the stiff material of her skirt. The clock ticks. The mottled rash that appears on her chest and neck whenever she is nervous rises. She does not know if it is from the years spent in her office, or whether her nerves have heightened the noise, but she can hear the ticking of the clock as if it's being held right next to her ear. *Tick-tock, tick-tock*. Someone in the front row sneezes; a burst of guttural laughter explodes from the raked seating; and all the while, *tick-tock, tick-tock*. The combination of two weeks of sleepless nights and two cups of coffee add to the trembling in her hands. He must be here, he must be in this room, but she is paralysed, unable to look. Finally, it is five past ten. With a gargantuan effort, with every fibre of her being telling her to run, she lifts her head, and begins to speak.

The relief is palpable, melting: the familiar warmth of success momentarily threatens collapse, an out-of-body experience. As the lights come up, her sight is crowded by dappled stars. A smile so wide that it hurts engulfs her face. She is amazed to look down and find hands still grasping the lectern, ten pink fingernails whitening at their tips from the pressure of the grip. Applause bursts out like an appreciative machine gun. A harried but smiling faculty member rushes up onto the stage to thank, green tweed, the faint smell of Old Spice, clasping hand shakes and apologetic thank yous. She is swept up in the tide of bodies moving down the aisle, papers still in hands, struggling elbows into sleeves, and all the while chatting, smiling, thanking, introducing. She is so caught up in the novelty of this euphoria that, turning back to shake the hand of an interested PhD student, she walks straight into him.

Laura's most vivid memory of Nathaniel is walking out of a bar near Marseille, her vision blurred by furious tears, looking back to see his lanky figure in its cotton slacks and striped shirt turning away from her. The summer after they finished their Masters: an idyllic three weeks in the South of France, sun, sand, sex, sailing, and, in this instance, the searing heartbreak of seeing him with someone else. Adultery, to her: scarcely worth mentioning, to him. She has thought since that 'adultery' was the wrong word: still hormone-driven, scarcely post-adolescent, they were barely adults. She doesn't think it would bother her now. But when she thinks of him, she thinks of that moment: the pout of annoyance, the frustration in his long face which is sure she will return, the half-empty drink in his hand. She remembers the long trudge back to the campsite, the convulsing fury that made it impossible to shove her belongings into a bag, the overwhelming urge to shout and scream and kick at anything in sight. She knew he didn't believe she would leave, but every step she took towards the station she was waiting for him to come running up to stop her. Even on the train, she was expecting him to suddenly appear in a declaration of love and devotion and repentance. She doesn't remember now exactly how she got back to England, but it was three days and hours upon hours of sobbing in French gares later. It was when she returned to her parents' home in Kent that the reality hit her. She didn't leave her bed for a week. But that was it. They'd met once, a month or so later, to exchange belongings. Nothing much was said. He didn't understand why she was being so unreasonable. She didn't think he would. And then, for a couple of years, the occasional post-card, a phone-call to catch up when the pain had dulled to a mere everyday presence, but in her head he was still the beautiful man in the bar annoyed with her hysterics.

Somehow the crowd around her melts away, drifts like smoke into the various corridors and down the stairways. After fifteen years of waiting, she doesn't know what to say. The man in front of her is tall, but greyer now; the engaging green eyes have bags; the politician's smile is worn. She is frozen, not knowing whether to kiss his cheek or shake his hand. Instead, they stand in the corridor: two strangled teenagers in bodies approaching middle age.

"Hello."
She is pleased to be the first to speak.
"Hello."

A pause that can be cut with a knife. She cannot move her mouth, she is too busy searching his face, the freckles and scars and dimples flood her with familiarity after all this time. When finally found, their words come all at once, a rush of "You look wonderful" and "It's great to see you" and "Shall we get a coffee?" and "I know a place just around the corner"...

She has always secretly imagined that their eventual meeting would be momentous, a moment of all-engulfing passion, a scene from Breakfast at Tiffany's or Singing in the Rain. In reality, it is not. In reality, it is awkward. In reality, fifteen years have done a lot to sepia-coat and rose-tint her memories into photographic perfection. They sit in a table in the window, not in a seductively smoky bar or a quaint little café, but in Café Nero, surrounded by people half their age using more communication devices than Laura has ever seen. Laptops, mobiles, headsets, pagers – apparently no one has conversations any more. He has a skinny macchiato: she feels staid with a cup of tea. The day outside is cold and grey. She can see traces of condensation building up around the edging of the window. Outside, people shoot past in various states of hurry, haste and glumness. Inside, there is music in the background, the crashing of trays, the hissing of machines and the shouting of baristas. She can feel his foot tapping incessantly under the table. They twitch nervously – two cups and a shared biscuit between two adolescent adults past their prime all there is to show for the romance of a lifetime. They talk. He is married, a wife and two small children; a house in Hammersmith and a mortgage that's breaking his back; an estate car and trips to her parents in Hampshire or Ikea at the weekends. She talks about Jeffrey; the house; the garden she never really goes into.

Children? Oh, no, it was never the right time. It's funny, he's always imagined her with children. She stares into her cup. There is a pause. A pause that speaks words, that speaks years. He looks at her. She looks out of the window. Something is beginning to hurt, a clagginess in the back of her throat that vibrates with the noise and bustle of the coffee shop. He clears his throat.

"Laura..."

She shakes her head. Her throat is heavy now, pregnant with the tears of so much regret, so much *stupid* regret that she wants to hit herself for never having done anything about it. It is too late. He walks her to her bus stop, and then up to Holborn. She concentrates on the ground under her feet, the greyness of the paving with its lines and grime and years of chewing gum stamped into the stone. She can't feel her body any more. It is as if she is made of air. At the entrance to the station, in one last attempt to turn back time, she flings her arms around him in a gesture as futile as it is foolish. She is astonished that she can feel his heart beating through so many layers of coat. She wants to stay there, her face against him, his smell, his touch, the mingling of salty tears with the fine wool.

And then, somehow, she goes.

She is not controlling her legs as they walk her through the barrier, or down the escalator, or on to the train. Her neck does not let her turn back. Her ears block out the sound of his last words as she walks away for a second time.

She cries all the way home, not the violent sobs of youth but the silent, steady flow of tears that seems to stream from the crushing of her heart. She gets off the train a stop early and steps out into the bright winter light, desperate to breathe, but her lungs will not accept the air. She is desperate to breathe. She walks, up and down rows upon rows of terraced streets, past builders, buggies, cars and old ladies. She sways. She leans on a wall to catch her breath, to try and chase the air into her enfeebled lungs. Her stomach is empty; her body seems nothing more than skin and bones stretched around a hollow hole. She retches, but the bile in all its lurid glory won't tease itself out from beyond the back of her throat. She wonders if it will be there forever. She sees her face in a window, gaunt, streaked and oddly white given the rawness of the salt on her skin.

A wind is whipping along these streets. The leafless trees shake their frail arms in protest. On the high street one man's umbrella inverts itself, and a plastic bag rises majestically into the ether. Laura looks up, trying to see with her eyes this invisibility that whistles round her ears and pounds at her back. It is a Chinese dragon swimming through the air, darting between buildings, arching its back in regal waves and whipping pedestrians with its whiskers. As she watches its unseen progress and lilts in the wake of its tail, part of her seems to rise with it. Bustled on the pavement, she feels like a bird soaring high, high up and away: in her mind's eye she can see the tiny, ant people hurrying about their daily life, and bug cars hooting and tooting along the crowded roads. It all seems terribly comic.

Somewhere between the organic grocer's and her front door, she stops crying. It is not a conscious decision, but either from the exhaustion or the all-prevailing need for self-preservation, her body says, "enough". The transition from the cold outdoors to the warm hallway burns her ears and tingles the tips of her fingers. She is greeted by the sight of Jeffrey's concentrated peeling of potatoes in the kitchen.

"How was it, love?"

"It was fine, really fine."

"Dinner at six?"

"Lovely."

Slowly her feet take her up the stairs, the soft, familiar carpet squidging between toes that have been cramped into someone else's shoes all day. She passes the familiarities, the prints and lithographs and wall hangings – *Crystal Palace and the Great Exhibition*, Durer's *Hare*, a dark northern factory… The soft beige of her bedroom envelops her in cotton wool. She takes off the high-necked jumper, the stiff skirt, and climbs into a dressing gown so thick it could almost be a human embrace. Lying on her bed, staring at the ceiling, the 'pip-pip' of Radio Four downstairs, the tapping of shoes on the kitchen floor. She will never see him again. The whirling of all these last words in her head: Laura, love, dinner, leave. Her eyes are heavy, a shadowy deity presses leaden weights into them. She is tired. Just terribly, terribly tired... But, she tells herself, it is fine. Nothing lasts forever. This pain won't last forever. In a few days it will already be old; a few weeks, the occasional stab; a few months, hardly anything at all. Life will go on, minutes, into hours, into days, and beyond. Tomorrow, they will have faded, but tonight, she will have to listen to these words.

Laura. Love. Dinner. Leave.
Laura. Love. Dinner. Leave.

And his final word.
Goodbye.

Johnny

by Laura Hocking

So it was an average Saturday night. Perhaps not everyone's average, but the usual routine: going round to Lenny's, making as much headway through his beer and records as I can and then, when the fun runs out, walking back home across town. Sometimes Lenny has the girls over – he always calls them that even when they're not specifically ours – usually crazy ones that you wouldn't want to talk too much to, but they look nice sitting there cross-legged on the carpet, pouring their beers into glasses and gossiping about fashion and Marx and all the empty speculation that rolls over you nice and comfortable with a few beers inside. That night, the conversation had been particularly wild, retrospeccing on the latest gigs and cabaret shows and suchlike, and the girls taking turns to stand up and redo their favourite moments from the shows and taking off their shoes and laughing with their heads thrown back, when Lenny announced that it was time for us to leave. It was probably getting on for Sunday by that time, and you can't blame a guy like Lenny for wanting to spend a Sunday morning with a girl like Christine, and some of the other girls were yawning too, so we packed them into a couple of taxis and paid the drivers upfront and sent them off into the dark. Now if I had the money to be catching my own taxis at the end of the night I'd probably be moving in circles that would exclude me from the likes of Lenny and his songbird bobbysoxers, but as it was I found myself walking alone in December, down the wide, dark streets of Moscow or Boston or wherever you think I might have been walking at four a.m. on a Sunday morning, after a night of beer and girls.

So it's cold, and it's dark, the streetlighting's not up to much even though they charge you extra over your rent for it, and I'm walking along with only a thin overcoat and no scarf, and I'm really very cold. So I'm walking fast. Not because I'm scared of the dark, or because I'm wondering if someone will just pop out of the darkness and start on me, though god knows I might be scareder if I thought I looked like I was worth robbing, but it's clear from the jacket. It's a thready old army jacket, the real thing. Not a vintage knockoff you get for a week's wages in the silver-spoon bohemia, no, it's the real thing. A guy in a youth hostel gave it to me. Imagine it: he tells me he's got something terminal and then hands me his jacket, saying it won't be cold where he's going and I don't mean to rain on the poignancy of the transaction, but it was a youth hostel in Norway in February, pissing icicles almost, and I couldn't think why he wouldn't want to make the rest of his life as cosy as he could. But when I found myself wearing that thin old army jacket in December I realised that he hadn't sacrificed as much as I'd thought.

It's an interesting story as to why I was in Norway in the first place, and I can truthfully say that I couldn't explain if you asked me. I couldn't remember. A few months ago, maybe a year now, I went walking under some scaffolding when some son of a builder nudged his lunchbox off the planking. It doesn't sound like much, but he was sat up on the second storey with a thermos full of christknows, and it's a miracle I have a head at all. I remember it all clear as Christmas, well enough to give an interview in the local press and make poster boy for public safety, but since that point things have been a little shoddy. There are plenty of stories about people getting into car crashes or falling down ravines and coming up with blind amnesia and suchlike, but the truth is that I can remember better than before. If anything I find it hard to forget things. Silly stuff like exactly how many times the phone rang last time Lenny called, or what colour socks my sister wore when we had that argument on the beach about her smashing up the barnacles with a spade for no conceivable reason.

Maybe it looks like things have picked up for me, that I've turned into some kind of superman since that embarrassing occurrence under the scaffold, but I have to say I just don't feel superb about it. My head's a filing cabinet all full of notes, but you know a filing cabinet can't run itself, it needs a secretary or a clerk or someone to make sure all the slips go in the right files so that if someone comes into the office and says 'I need to know what Josephine thinks about music, do you have any conversations on file?' then your secretary can just dive right in and find you exactly what you need before you've even finished the question.

So my secretary's gone off with a lunchbox, and that's the end of the interesting story about why I was in Norway. I remember planning to go for a long time, and buying a rucksack, and that when I was there I met a girl, but I'm not so sure how the facts relate. I can presume that I probably bought a rucksack because I wanted to go to Norway, that would be a practical thing to say, but as for the impulse that made me want to go, or whether I knew the girl would be there and that's why I went – I'm drawing blanks. She was very tall, short black hair and a big mouth and I remember that we slept together a few times and that I left without telling her. I don't know how it links up.

Sometimes I wonder if that's what it was like for the army guy, the one who gave me the jacket. He said he was in a war once, though I'm hazy on which one because the details he gave made no fucking sense. He was a very old guy, so it could have been any of them. I remember his words, but the meaning's gone a bit to seed in transit. He talked a lot about the dark, and how dark it was at night time and how even in the day time it was like you were wearing dark glasses. He just talked fudge mostly, but if you said any sort of word like *dark* or *cold* or if he asked if there was someone in the toilet and you said it was *empty*, he'd start on a long and generally repetitious conversation with himself about how nobody can really know what words like that mean. *Hungry*, as well, he told me he'd hit me if I said it out loud. Mostly I just let him talk, because he seemed to like it, and also because I used to be quite a dreamy sort of person according to Lenny, and I'd have come up with something vague in reply and he'd have gone off on another argument.

So I'm walking down the dark, flat Boulevard de Rochechaourt – but down in the scrubby end, with the guys shouting 'Marlboromarlboromarlboro' till you can't recognise it, not up by the red light district where Brits will pay 200 Euros to get into the Moulin Rouge – and I'm counting the strips of concrete between the paving slabs and trying to remember what it might have felt like to be scared of the dark. There's a Jamaican guy hanging about in a doorway looking shifty, so I ask him if he's got a light, just to make conversation, and he backs off and starts walking really fast, so I figure that if I could remember how to be scared, then that would probably have scared me. Even if I'm wearing a rough old army jacket and looking worn, I'm not so big of a man, and if a big Jamaican like him was scared of me, then it makes sense that I ought to be scared of what other sorts of people I might bump into on the Boulevard de Rochechaourt. So I go on, taking a squander over my shoulder to see if there's anyone around that I might want to fear, when I walk right bang into this girl. I trod on her foot completely and she gave a little oink of pain and said 'putain!' the way they do. There was a bus shelter there spilling a bit of orange light over her and the shutter she was leaning up against and we got a good look at each other. I can tell you truthfully that she was the ugliest girl alive. When you think that I can remember the faces of all the girls I've seen since my mishap then it's nothing to laugh at. She had some genuinely horrific hair that stuck out for six inches on either side of her head in a big frizzed halo, and I suppose she'd broken her nose at some point, possibly upon exiting the womb because it looked pretty unfixable from where I was standing. Her lips hung too big on her tiny chin so it looked like half her face had got wet and fallen off. Even her eyes weren't that nice, just small and dark and a bit dry.

It wasn't that I felt sorry for her, but it was as close to pity as I could come. I figured that with that sort of a face she wouldn't get much, and I hadn't had any since the girl in Norway, so maybe we'd be compatible. She might even be grateful. I'm not so good at loving. I know that if there's a word for it then it must have a meaning. At one point I knew what it was and that's probably something to do with Norway, but I've lost it. Maybe it's lost me. I don't get ruffled. I can fudge it if needs be, and the flipside is that when it doesn't go right then I don't really care. It can be convenient, like when you need to dispatch a flattened cat.

So we're eyeing each other up, this girl and I, and it's one of those pauses that's too long to be entirely comfortable, so I ask her if she wants a smoke and she says no. Now I can only think that this much be a touch of panic on her part, because I can see from her teeth that she's a smoker, and you can smell it too. I guess it must have got into her skin or something, because the clothes looked pretty fresh, in fact, she looked like she'd just put them on five minutes ago, like maybe she'd been expecting me. When someone turns down a smoke it's hard to know what to do. You're left standing there offering the packet with a cigarette nudged out all ready, and the only credible thing you can do is put it between your own lips and light it. Except as you'll remember I don't have a lighter. I said back then that I was only asking for conversational purposes, which is true because the fact was that I didn't have the yen for a smoke at the time of asking, though if I had I would have had to ask all the same because I'd given my new clipper to one of Lenny's girls to use and she must have forgotten it in her pocket or something.

'Tu as du feu?' I asked, but she got all pink in the face, more like orange in that light, and she blushed and tried to indicate that she wasn't French. I thought that was a funny bit of happenstance, because she swore in perfect French, and I hadn't banked on her being anything other than a genuine French whore. I worked that one out from the lipstick. Why else would you mock a face like that by putting lipstick on it? We'd been standing around all pricked and pickled for a while, swapping words in broken French when we'd both have been happier in sign language, then she made like she was going to go back to leaning against the shutter so I grabbed her arm and said 'Tu travailles ce soir?' She didn't know what I was talking about, which is thick, really, because you'd expect them to give her a brief education before they set her out there like a Christmas tree when she can't even recognise a customer if comes up and offers her a smoke. I tried again, 'Combien?' and made the money sign with my fingers. Everybody knows the money sign.

The girl was opaque, truly, and not even just of low intelligence but really lacking in the sort of common sense that most stupid people still manage to hold on to. Do you know what? She actually reached down into a little pocket in the side of her skirt, took out two Euros and put it into my hand. I might not be able to put things together quite right all the time, but I can't think of anyone else who'd be thick enough to do that.

So it's not that I was *feeling* angry, not as such, but I thought that it was probably time somebody taught her a lesson. Educated her on a certain register of French vocabulary. I stepped a little closer, till I could smell her breath.

'Travailler.' I said, and made the digging action with both hands. I couldn't really think of any other professions to illustrate, except maybe for a builder, but I didn't want her to think I was a mime act so I stopped at that.

'Feu.' I curled my fingers into my palm and clicked my thumb pad over my trigger finger knuckle. I held the invisible lighter to the tail of my cigarette, which was still stuck in the corner of my mouth, and pretended to smoke it.

'Combien?' For this one, I took my wallet out of my pocket and pretended to pull out notes from the stash of twenties that I hadn't had in a long time. Her piggy eyes widened at the sight of the wallet, which made me more sure than ever that she was a whore, and I snapped it shut.

'Morte.' I reached back into the back pocket of my jeans, and made a great show of extracting the screwdriver.

I think I should take this opportunity to tell you about this screwdriver, because at one point it must have meant a lot to me. When I was younger, before I came here and fell in with Lenny, of course, I had a little friend called Giles. Giles was English, but the wrong kind of English, and he was constantly getting picked on for his stupid name, and his cup-of-tea accent and for all sorts of funny ways and manners that didn't go down well. You'd think California was a nice place, full of sun-loving hippies and suchlike, but it's not like that everywhere and all the time. I won't even go into the reasons why I left, and where I got the money, and what that might have had to do with Norway, because if you find out you'll want to pass it on to someone else, and then they'll tell two more people and before I know it I'll be on a slow boat to nowhere.

Giles was forever getting jumped on, and losing his lunch money and all sorts of stupid shit, and naturally enough he got tired of submitting to the general routine of getting squashed, recovering, and getting squashed again. So what Giles did was he bought himself a screwdriver. I was there when he got it, down at the hardware place, told the guy he had an art project or something but he picked it out specially for its weight. It was a heavy old screwdriver with a great solid wood handle and tracks carved in for grip, biggest one he could find. He took it into Technology class one day when the teacher was off doing something he shouldn't have been, and sharpened the screwdriver on a grinding wheel till it glowed. He cut his shorts just pocketing it. That was the point, for everyone to see Giles sharpening this *weapon*, to see him putting it into his shorts like he did it every day, and then hopefully nobody would come and pulp him again. Giles was a smart one and I won't tell you that it didn't work because it did. So the screwdriver has sentimental value because it might have saved Giles' life if he hadn't been green enough to sleep with the first girl who offered. He picked up something nasty and fair shot himself in the head out of shame. He was Jewish, but I don't know if that has anything to do with it.

This girl was looking more skittish by the minute when she saw the thing glinting in the light from the bus shelter, but I swear she was too slow even to scream, let alone run away. She had serious problems processing reality. She was just looking at it like she didn't recognise the object, so I raised it up to shoulder height and made a great show of stabbing her and doing the music from *Psycho*. Then I dragged one finger across my throat to further the explanation of *morte*. I suppose I had her quite hard back against the shutters, and I could feel her breath all over my face and I found it quite disgusting. I hadn't realised I could still go in for disgust, even if only on a practical level, but that's exactly what was going through my head. She didn't seem to be enjoying my dumb-show so far, and I was getting tired of waiting for a reaction. I said 'putain' a few times, pointing at her, and she seemed to get that one, but to be frank it's tiring just being near someone who's too thick to understand when you're pretending to stab them, let alone trying to create social intercourse. I had half a mind to teach her *violer*, but there were other people in the street, granted not the sort of people that would have stopped me, but the kind that would have asked me for money afterwards, and all I'd have would be her 2 Euros.

It was at this point that I started hitting her. I don't really know why I bothered because she was not someone you could have knocked sense into, but as I said it was very cold and quite dark, and I wanted to see if I could feel anything other than disgust. So I slapped the ugliest side of her face with the palm of my left hand, connecting bang in the middle of her chubby cheek. Her head veered off to one side, and I slapped it back central with the back of the same hand. Maybe that was excessive, my knuckle caught her just under her beady little eye and left a big red mark that quickly purpled over and looked like it might be throbbing. Finally, she started to scream, full-on screaming right in my ear as though that would drive away a little guy in an army jacket with one hand full of screwdriver and the other singing with the impact of her face. There aren't even words for how stupid that is, but I guess one of us had to run and since I could see this big black guy hanging out of a window three floors up with a face like death and a kitchen knife, I supposed it should be me.

The Amphibians

by Claire Lowdon

Sid and Robby didn't like the same shops. Sid's pace would slow when they passed estate agents, or building societies advertising competitive ISAs, or electrical goods stores. Robby was more interested in the weird fruits the barrow boys were selling and the latest releases at Blockbuster and the pic'n'mix in the newsagent's window.

At this stage of the journey Robby had to speed up with a tripping hop if he wanted to get a proper look at the fruit or the sweets or the videos. He'd just snatch a glimpse before Sid's long legs in their neatly creased suit trousers would cut across the busy window like curtains at the theatre, and he'd have put on another spurt to get past them. Sid, on the other hand, liked this bit of the walk because it was flat and he could stride cleanly and quickly without his hip playing up as it soon would on the hill up to the station. Robby's skipping irritated him, but he never told him to look where he was going because he didn't want Robby to think that he couldn't cope with holding his hand whilst he bobbed about like that.

Robby wished his grandfather wouldn't walk so fast but he knew that before long he'd be the fast one. He could always tell when Sid's leg started to hurt because of the way his eyes would narrow for just a split second each time he stepped with it. Robby knew exactly how to time his walking so he slowed down at the same rate as Sid. It was his game never to be even half a paving stone ahead. If they reached the top together, he'd won the race. Except he wasn't racing Sid; he was racing himself. It was all about timing.

Robby didn't like the dirty grey dog that belonged to the man begging on the corner, so Sid always walked on the left on the way there and the right on the way back, to be between Robby and the dog.

Sid and Robby went swimming every Thursday, and it was always about five to four by the time they got to Archway tube station. This was because Sid still ran things by his wristwatch exactly as he had done when he was in the navy. He even kept a log book, and encouraged Robby to do likewise; he was a proper grandfather, even if Robby wasn't that interested in the navy and couldn't be bothered to write a log. And as soon as they reached the station, Sid would always put his hand in his coat pocket and give Robby *two* of the sherbert lemons that Robby wasn't meant to have since his filling. Sid didn't trust the ticket machines, so they always bought their two returns to Highgate please from the woman in the booth.

One of the hardest bits of the journey was the escalator. It was on an escalator that the shiny metal joint inside Sid's hip had once popped out in a screamingly painful way, which was why taking the escalator was at once very dangerous and very important to Sid. Getting the escalator right was all about timing, too. They had to make sure that there wasn't anybody straight in front of them, so that Sid would have all the space he needed when they got off at the bottom, but especially that there wasn't anybody for quite some way behind them, so that Sid could take as long as he wanted to at the top.

Robby would never get on first. He'd made that mistake once and he'd been halfway down by the time Sid had managed to get safely onto the top steps. Then he'd remembered what his dad had told him about how dangerous it was for Sid to take the escalators when Robby was the only one with him, and how they should always, always use the lift, and he'd run back up the escalator as fast as he could. He reached Sid just as he was getting to the bottom, in time to take his arm and ask him worriedly whether he was alright. Sid was angry with him for asking that; he said of course he was alright and did Robby take him for a fool or what. But every time after that they waited together at the top for the perfect moment before getting on, even if it took as long as five minutes. The waiting was always done in silence, and they always thought pretty much the same thoughts whilst they waited.

Sid thought about how patient Robby was with him, and how he, Sid, could never have been that patient at his age or even twenty years ago. He wondered what Robby was thinking, whether Robby minded waiting like this, and whether Robby compared the Sid he saw now with the young man Sid told him about who had once been the most fearless of men in the most fearsome of sea storms. Sid certainly made that comparison, every Thursday. But Robby wasn't thinking about sea storms or even younger Sids. He was thinking only about Sid-now, and how funny it was that love for Sid-now stopped him from ever mentioning the lift, even though that would have been much safer for his grandfather. And most of all, he was thinking how funny it was that his dad almost certainly wouldn't understand any of this if he ever tried to explain it to him.

On the tube, Sid always sat and Robby always stood. Often there were enough seats for both of them to sit, but Robby liked trying to keep his balance without holding on, and Sid never insisted that he stop mucking around. If the tube was very empty Robby would swing round the pole in middle. He'd wrench himself back and forth in great arcs that brought him closer to Sid's face each time, until Sid would have to jerk his head back to get out the way, and Robby would laugh and stop. Much later, the baked-bean smell of stale coffee on his own breath would remind him of swinging up to his grandfather's similar private stench on the underground, followed immediately by the relief of swooping back into cleaner air.

Today there was a man with an enormous beer gut standing up too, leaning heavily against the glass panel at the end of the row of seats Sid was sitting on. He was wearing a black t-shirt that turned the glass into a dark mirror of squashed belly. Sid could see himself quite clearly, with Robby dipping in and out of the background. He thought again how his ears were the same as Robby's ears, almost oblong with lobes that took up just a bit too much space. He thought of his son's neat ears, with their oddly sensitive, fuzzy coating of tiny, soft white hairs, and his small pale hands. He wondered how much the fact that he and his grandson had the same ears had to do with how much he liked Robby. Then he caught himself wondering that and realised what nonsense it was and remembered to focus on the journey.

The swimming baths were very close to East Finchley tube station. Sid and Robby both had membership cards, so they didn't have to pay. All they needed was twenty pee each for the lockers, and Sid always remembered to bring that. Happily inhaling the soporific smell of the chlorine, they simultaneously (Sid above, Robby below) pushed open the swing door into the strip-lit men's changing room with its comforting low burble of male voices. This was their place. It felt safe and routine and they were both relieved to have got there.

It was pretty much the same as the changing room at the baths Robby went to with school, only getting changed here with Sid was completely different from getting changed there. There, he and everyone else could see that his freckles carried on from his face all over his whole body, which was a lot smaller than most of the other boys'. But Robby knew that Sid was even more uncomfortable changing than he was. He wasn't quite sure why, because most of the other older men were *too* comfortable, and walked round talking to each other with everything drooping around down there. Sid always turned to face the wall whilst he undressed, and didn't turn round until he had his scratchy brown and orange towel tucked tightly round his waist in a neat skirt. Even then, Robby thought he could tell that his grandfather was embarrassed of what his skin did now that it was wearing out.

At the lockers, Sid's fingers with their lined nails fumbled the twenty pee into the slot. It was always Sid who did the money and Robby who put the clothes in. Once he'd done that he put his verruca sock in too. Sid never suggested he wear it.

Sid hated the next bit, because he knew he'd have to take Robby's arm at some point. It was stepping down into the cold grey footbath you had to walk through to reach the pool that was the problem. There was no handrail. The first time Sid had just lifted his elbow onto Robby's shoulder to steady himself as subtly as possible, but he'd put more weight onto Robby than he'd intended to and the boy almost lost his footing. Now Sid gripped Robby's forearm, the two of them holding their joined arms between and in front of them as though they were carrying something that might spill. The trick was to go slowly and concentrate on balancing rather than leaning. Sid thought how odd it was that Robby was so much better at doing things slowly than he was. He sort of felt it should be the other way round. His son was good at doing things slowly too, but somehow that was different.

Today, the walk from the footbath to the pool steps was fine, because the bobbly tiles were dry. Robby jumped in floppily so as not to hit the bottom of the shallow end and Sid eased himself down the steps, front first. Here they were, together in the same grey cube of water and dirty yellow light, where none of the other swimmers – dark hairy men, rubber-hatted old women, skinny girls with wrinkled cozzies – would want to talk to them, and where it wasn't the same as on land, and where all that mattered was moving your body around in the nicest possible ways. Sid and Robby loved swimming.

Sid would begin by bending his long legs so his knees went out to the sides, and he'd hover in that frog-shape with his body under up to his neck, the water slapping at the bottom of his hair and turning the pale grey wisps into heavy black strands. He pushed his hands out in front of him and made tiny breast-stroke circles in order to stay in the same place. Sometimes Robby would try to copy this, but he wasn't tall enough, and he'd end up falling forwards or tipping into full-on breaststroke. So whilst Sid 'accustomed himself' to the water, Robby would pace up and down the wriggling black lines on the bottom of the pool like a tight-rope walker, arms out horizontally. Once they'd both got used enough to the water for their goose-bumps to disappear, Sid and Robby would look at each other and Robby would count – *one... two...* THREE! – and they'd both put their heads under at exactly the same moment, sharing the sharp initiation of shivering neck-seize.

The Rhythm of Black Lines

by Benjamin Morris

A friend of mine tells me she wants one of my poems embroidered on her panties. This is fine with me, but not only is there the question of her boyfriend, it is also a fairly long poem, some two hundred lines or so, and there is no way the whole thing will fit.

She shrugs. "So I'll put the parts I like best."

"You can't put just part of it," I cry out. "The whole thing is knit together line by line. It would be like pulling a leg off a dog!"

My friend likes dogs, so I know I have scored a point. But still we have not resolved how the poem will fit on her panties.

On the second floor of the dry-cleaners there is a lady to whom my mother has been bringing clothes for years. She is one of those soft Southern fixtures whom Harper Lee would probably describe as 'all frosted over with sweat and sweet talcum,' but nevertheless she is a wizard with hems and alterations. I have never actually seen this wizard, electing to stay in the car whenever my mother took in shirts or trousers or sport coats, so I am a little hesitant as I enter the shop. At the sound of the bell Mr. Enfield, the owner, a self-described Republican 'back when it weren't in style to be one,' hobbles to the front.

"Why, young Brady," he hollers, a little hoarse, as usual. "What'd you scuff up today?" Mr. Enfield is always exceedingly friendly to me, but I never really know what to say to him. Heaven knows my usual lead of the latest story on public radio won't work – if there's one thing he can't stand, it's 'them dad-blasted libbuls on that got-dog talk-box.' I have been down this road before.

"Oh, nothing, Mr. Enfield," I say. "Just something for Miss Ginger." I edge towards the stairwell to the left of the desk, trying less to conceal the pair of panties I am carrying than the sheets of paper whose lines, for some inauspicious reason, do not go all the way across the page.

"Right, well, be on with you, then," he dismisses me with a wave. Mr. Enfield's arm doesn't go up as high as it used to, so his wave looks more like he is stroking an invisible cat.

The carpeting on the stairs has long since worn away, and the bulb hanging down from the rafter fizzes and pops as I pass underneath it. I wonder how Miss Ginger (if she even is a Miss – I don't know what she is) hasn't fried a small furrow into her hair. Then I wonder if, having gone up, she has ever come back down. At the top the landing curves back behind me, and I follow a narrow, winding hallway whose tapioca-colored wallpaper has never known natural light. After a moment I reach one of those fake teak doors split in the middle so one can lean across the counter without actually entering a room. A sign reads: *~~Mrs~~ Ms Virginia Rawlings. Clothes and Fixings.* Gripping the panties and the poem, I knock.

There is a silence. Then I hear a sound as though someone within is rocking their chair steadily towards the door, back and forth, inch by inch. Then the top half of the door opens and I am face to face with Ms Virginia.

"Hi, Ms Ginger," I begin, "I'm Mrs. Brady's son."

She squints at me, hard, then her face softens into recognition and she smiles sweetly. She is about as old as I had imagined, full to plumpness of matronly love and marzipan, and instantly I fear this business I have to work with her will not be easy.

"Come on in, hon'," she says. "Would you like a snickerdoodle?" From atop a portable television set playing

Jack Benny reruns she takes a plate of warm, cinnamon-sugar speckled cookies.

Now, of course, it is too late. With such an offer in play it is too late to turn back, too late to find someone whose only connection to me on this earth consists of these unfortunate lines and their unholy receptacle. Not snickerdoodles, not politics, and especially – *especially* – not my mother.

"Why, they're my favorite kind," I say with a grin, and taking one, bite down, slow and full, into the still-moist core of the cookie. It may well be the saddest cookie I have ever eaten.

"And how's your mother?" The word comes out *mutha*.

"She's just fine," I say, still chewing. "Says to tell you hello. Hot one we're having out there today, ain't it?"

"Oh, ain't that the truth," she says, "My gardenias are liketa shrivel up and stop smelling if we don't get a lick anytime soon."

I nod knowingly, and mumble something into the snickerdoodle about gerbera daisies and the tuft of lamb's ear we've just planted.

"Well, what can I do you for? Don't tell me you're bringing in those same corduroys I've patched up so many times… Lord, I know those pants better than you do!" She gets a little tickled at the thought, and I reckon I better jump in while the water's warm.

"I need your help with something kind of unusual, Ms Ginger," I say. "I've got this friend, and she had this idea, and… well, how good is your needlework? I mean, not for repairs or anything, but for the fine stuff, you know, detail work."

"Dear," she says, and levels at me, "I could thread a cat's eye without it blinking."

"Then we may be in business," I say. "I need someone to put this" – I lift the six pages of poem text – "on this." I set the panties, white cotton Maidenform size 5, on the split in the door.

Ms Ginger seems to lose a little of the lustre in her face, though whether at the goods or the task, I can't tell.

"Oh," she says. "My."

I give an apologetic half-smile and leave the items there, for her to warm to the idea, for it to soak in. At the moment she looks as though her propriety has taken her by the arm and is gently leading her away from the deed; but embarrassed and reluctant as I am to prolong her discomfort, I am still in need of her craftsmanship.

"You can name your rate, if you like." At this she briefly lifts her gaze from what must by now be a heathen altar on which rests the lowing sacrifice. Now the idea has grown hooks, is taking hold. Past her on the wall is a calendar spilling over with pictures of fat toddlers smearing cake all over their faces like dirt, and this gives me an idea.

"Set your price," I say, "and you can buy your grandkids as many overalls as you please."

But I have miscalculated, have not seen the desert for the sand: she gives a short, wheezy laugh, and looks me square in the eye. "A seamstress never buys what she can stitch by hand, darlin'." Her words drip out like sweet tea sat too long.

Sheepish, I nod, and take the poem and the panties and crumple them up in one hand. I try to effect as graceful a retreat as possible: I thank her for her time, allow again how unusual of a request it is, and step back from the door. As I go I do not mention my mother, though I fear by the time I have reached my car there will be a certain kind of message on my home answering machine.

Before descending the stairs I turn and face the landing. "Thank you for the snickerdoodle," I call back.

There is a place across town that I know also does alterations. While I am driving there, a story comes on public radio about what happens to different kinds of cargo when freighters shipwreck in the middle of their voyage. Apparently after their containers decompose the ocean currents will take the sneakers or ping-pong balls, or, in this case, rubber duckies, and carry them all over the world. There are actually groups in over sixty countries dedicated to charting the passage of these inadvertent seafarers.

"I have seen the little duckies three whole times," says one amateur oceanographer from Iceland. He sounds as though he is tromping through somebody else's consonant patch. "We throw the nets and take them from the water. Then we paint them green and put them back. That is how we know they are the same."

The reporter is talking about sighting parties held on various continents when I pull into the shopping center. I wonder what it must be like, hundreds of people bundling happily up on the freezing Icelandic shore, just to maybe glimpse a bright green rubber ducky pass near the rocks. What happens if one founders? Or beaches? Does some brave, noble soul shuck off all his clothes to swim out and save it? Do they receive an Order of Merit? What if a freighter full of panties capsized? How far would they go?

I am still wondering, a little sadder now, as I enter the craft shop. Navigating through the aisles I finally find the desk for fabric alterations, which is deserted except for a very weary girl sitting behind the desk. As I approach she does not look up at me.

"Hi," I say.

"One second, please." She is filling out a form. While she writes I take the chance to steal a glance at her. Kathryn, for that is her name, is actually quite pretty, at least I imagine she would be if she weren't wearing a shop uniform clearly designed to flatten curves, dull edges, and dim lights. She has auburn hair, lovely jade eyes, and a close-set mouth whose lipstick has nearly worn away for all the times today she has pursed her lips.

After a moment she finishes her form, signs it, and slaps it on a nearby spike.

"It feels really good to do that," she says.

"Yeah," I say. "I know."

"Sometimes I write out receipts for things like pomegranates, just so I can slap them on there."

"Mm," I reply.

"We're a craft shop. We don't carry pomegranates."

"That's too bad," I say, "I like pomegranates."

She eyes me. "I don't usually trust people who like pomegranates, but I'm willing to make an exception. It depends, of course, on how much work you have for me to do."

"Well," I clear my throat, and look around the store.

"Uh-oh," she says. "I'm not seeing any exceptions in your future."

"It's not that it's a lot of work," I say, shifting the poem and the panties in my hands. "I mean, it is, but it's interesting work. At least, I think so."

"This morning I stitched a baby flamingo onto the back of a Hell's Angels jacket. If you can top that, you've got your exception." She smiles, and I think I feel the ink on the poem start to run in my palm.

"Okay," I say, and place my cargo on the desk. "I need this poem embroidered on these panties."

At this Kathryn's eyes gleam like little stars which have just been born. She grabs the underwear from me and holds it up to the light, testing the thin cotton in her fingers.

"Color or black and white?"

"Pardon?"

"The thread. How visible do you want this text? Do you want to be able to read it from a distance, or should you have to get... up close?" She smiles again, and I think I may have earned my exception.

"I don't honestly know," I say. This is not something my friend and I had covered. "I'm mostly worried about the length. It's an awfully long poem to go on a pair of panties."

Kathryn nods. "It is, isn't it." She runs her hand over the underwear, smoothing it out on the desk. Behind me a woman and her teenage daughter have joined the line, and I feel a slight, creeping blush which I am amazed has not surfaced before now. Kathryn's voice, while melodic, is by no means soft, and I cringe as she asks whether I would like my poem hand- or machine-stitched onto the panties.

"Can, er, it be done on a machine?" I ask, leaning forward and trying to whisper without appearing to do so.

"No, you're right," she says after a moment's consideration. From behind me I hear two delicate coughs, one after the other. "To fit the whole poem on there you'll need this to be done by hand. Let me think. I'm low on fine coloreds, so with black thread and a double stitch all around, how's next Thursday?"

I shrug. "Sure," I say. "You're sure you don't mind? Really, I wouldn't want to trouble you with such a time-consuming project if you have too much else to do."

I do not really believe this.

"Of course I don't mind," she says, and looks slyly – or is it coyly? – at me out of the corner of her eye. "This way I get to read someone else's poems for a change."

Days pass. I go to work, I come home, I read books and drink with friends. I plan a few poems, but do not actually write them. More days pass. My mother makes no mention of any calls from Ms Ginger, though I notice she knocks now before entering my room, which she never used to do. She knows I write poems, but, still.

"My manager didn't believe me when I told him it was a real order," sighs Kathryn the following week. "He's caught me using company machines for my own work before, and since you didn't sign an invoice there was no way I could convince him of the truth. If I give him one now he'll think I forged it. I'm so sorry." She seems genuinely disappointed.

"It's okay," I say. "What if I gave it to someone else here?"

She shakes her head. "I'm the best seamstress in the place save Ollie, who's lying in the hospital with prostate something-or-other. No one else would be up to the job."

"That's a pity," I say. "I hope he gets better soon."

"I do know somewhere else you can try," says Kathryn after a moment. "There's a place on Kennesaw Road, a little outside town on Old Highway 11, where I've sent people when we're too busy. They can be kind of cranky, but it's worth a shot. Tell them I sent you."

"Okay," I say. "Thanks."

"It was a wonderful poem, though," she says. "Would you like to go out on a date?" She asks this as easily as though she were asking the time.

"You move as fast as your needle, don't you," I say.

Kathryn smiles.

We decide on Japanese and a fireworks show which is to be held in the city park the following night. Mendenhall, as a town, tends to get very excited about the summer and takes it as an excuse to hold as many outdoor displays as will fit in its three short months, regardless of whether any national holidays are remotely on the horizon. So on any given night you can choose between fiddling concerts, public storytelling contests, discount skeet shooting, greased pig rodeos, or just about anything really. We pick fireworks because, having left the state some years ago, I haven't seen homegrown explosions in a very long time.

That afternoon I stop by the florist on the way home from work and pick up a white carnation, not too big, not too small. When I meet Kathryn at her apartment, she takes it and pins it in her hair, held up in a light silver clip, and kisses me happily on the cheek.

"My favorite bloom," she says, and we're off.

Later, bellies fat and happy with tempura and sashimi, we lie on a blanket and watch giant Ferris wheels and choo-choo trains and what could be chicken legs dissolve into the night sky. The blanket is one Kathryn has illicitly stitched on company equipment, a giant reproduction of a Piet Mondrian painting. I tell her it was too easy, that she should have tried a Chagall.

"Be quiet," she says. "This was one of my first. I'm working on a Klimt now."

I comply, and watch a massive sparkling bat make contact with a massive sparkling baseball. After what is surely an out-of-park home run they both melt softly away.

"Poems," says Kathryn, and turns to lie on her side to look at me. Her gaze is not uncomfortable, but for the moment I would rather take in chicken legs the size of nebulae than impromptu philosophical debate.

"Poems," I repeat. "I prefer writing them to reading them, but I'm not always so lucky."

"Good," she says. "Because I was worried."

"Why?"

"I don't know," she yawns. "Sometimes you find people who write poems just so they can say they write them. You didn't strike me as one of these, but I wanted to make sure."

"You know these people? I've never met any."

Kathryn laughs. "What backwoods, cricket-ridden swamp are you from?"

"This one?"

For a while we don't say anything. Every now and then one of our stomachs makes funny seafood noises, and neither of us mind. The fireworks are still going on, have been for an hour at least, and around us people are still shifting and settling like raindrops on an idling car. Some carry igloos full of sandwiches and booze, others drag toddlers behind them like unwilling pets, and still others content themselves to wander around and raise their beers to all their friends that have turned out for the show. Times like these, I think I like being at home. But not for too long – one can only watch so many chicken legs.

Kathryn tugs at my shirt. "Hey," she says.

I shift my weight a little and sit up on my elbows. She has inched a little closer, and is looking around as though she thinks she may recognize some of these people.

"Did you try the place on Old 11 for your panties?" she asks.

"They're not my panties."

Kathryn looks at me.

"Not yet," I say, "I meant to do it this afternoon but was too busy worrying about what to wear."

"And buying carnations," she adds, and smiles winningly.

My cheeks glow brighter than the fireworks. "I'll probably go tomorrow."

"Want me to come with? I can talk shop for you, if you like. Speak the scary needle-ese."

I grin. "Are you free after lunch?"

She thinks, and after a moment lets out a short sigh. "No, I'm not. Ollie's prostate swelled another two inches, and they've handed out all his shifts while they cut him open again. Damn. I totally forgot. I'm sorry."

"It's okay," I say. "I would have liked your help, but I can brave the wild jungles myself, I think."

"Next time?"

"Next time," I say. I have a momentary vision of thousands of bright green rubber ducks, bobbing obliviously along on the North Sea, looking like tasty little apples from below. Suddenly I want to know how many shark deaths from duck inhalation are reported each year.

"Sharks," I say. "How do you feel about sharks?"

She waits before responding. She appears to be

weighing several warring viewpoints in her mind. "I like them just fine," she says, finally, "in aquariums."

"The closest aquarium is in New Orleans," I say. "We could be there in three hours."

Kathryn has intent written all over her face.

The fireworks show is about over, and we stand to stretch, groaning luxuriously. As Kathryn stoops to fold the Mondrian I look idly around at others collecting their things, and to my surprise, and chagrin, I see Ms Ginger Rawlings about fifteen yards away with what must be her four grandchildren, all pleasantly plump from a surfeit of snickerdoodles, looking directly this way. She can hardly take her eyes off Kathryn. I wonder if they know each other through some seamstress' union, but then I realize that Ms Ginger is in fact making an assumption about whose undergarments it was that I brought her. Not only that, she seems to be making this assumption furiously.

When she sees me staring back at her she instantly drops her gaze and starts shooing her unruly little lambs along, toward the dirt parking lot. I laugh out loud at the sight of it, and resolve to listen to all the messages saved on my answering machine when I get home. *Lizabeth*, she'll have whispered into the phone, *I just had to tell you, saw your boy last night at the fireworks with some girl I didn't know*, and then the gossip train will have pulled out of the station, pure white panties waving out of every window.

On the drive out Old Highway 11 a follow-up story to the seafaring rubber duckies comes on the radio. I turn up the volume and settle comfortably into the seat of the Corolla. Apparently the story has generated so much interest that the news syndicate has had the reporter travel to the western coast of Ireland, where a number of these sightings take place due to the strong Atlantic currents. He has been interviewing residents of Galway, who by and large don't care too terribly much about the whole affair.

"I dinna see the fuss," says one elderly man, who has lived in the same cottage on the cliffs for eighty years.

"But don't you think it's a bit unusual to have flocks of flotsam floating by?" persists the reporter. Quickly he tries to contain his cleverness. "Surely this can't happen every day."

"It do," comes the reply. "Believe you me!"

"Can you explain what you mean?"

At this the gentleman just breaks into a great mysterious cackle. The reporter waits for him to finish, which he never really does, then moves onto a talkative young expat who describes once witnessing a flotilla of breast implants. The freighter carrying them had met an untimely end fifty miles north of Galway, and though the bulk of its cargo had sunk with it a few hundred implants still made it south on the waves.

"Who knows how they got here," says the young man, who is originally from Seattle. I can hear him beaming as he talks about the undulating silicone. "And who knows how they survived, chemically. But boy, was it beautiful. And sad. All those breasts-to-be."

The reporter lets the pathos sink in for a moment, the strains of a wild Irish flute echoing the young man's sorrow. The segment is almost up when he speaks to a survivor of one of these shipwrecks, a man from the Bahamas who used to work in the ship's mess and who has a lovely curl to his accent. The freighter he was on used to carry golf balls to historic Scottish courses, until one day a few years ago a freak storm came up near Islay and literally split his ship in half. They were close enough to shore that he and the rest of the crew were able to swim to safety, but this incident was enough to make him vow never to sail again. Still, he looks back on his days at sea with great fondness, he says. To pass the time they used to steal balls that had fallen loose from the crates and, using clubs an officer had smuggled on board, hit them off the deck into the ocean. They did this all the way across the Atlantic.

"Before we teed off we always marked them with our initials. Good luck charm," he says.

"And what were your initials?" the reporter asks.

"N.E.D.," says the man. "For Nathaniel Edward Dreyfus. But my mates called me Ned."

"Well, thank you, Ned," the reporter says. "Maybe you'll see one of your golf balls again one day."

"I already have," says Nathaniel Edward Dreyfus, "I already have."

Gritty Ricky's Bait and Stitch Shop sits on a bend in Kennesaw Road right off Old 11, sharing a building with a Shell station and Dan's Dinner, a restaurant whose name has always made me wonder. The parking lot is mostly empty, though a few truckers shuffle and gnaw on fat cigarettes as they fill up their hundred-gallon tanks.

Once inside I carry the poem and the panties to where Ricky, an enormous bald man with a fiery orange goatee, sits purling a scarf. Around me hang racks and racks of fishing tackle and cross-stitched samplers of imagined schoolhouses, and decorating all the walls are newspaper clippings and photos of when Ricky used to be a prize fighter on the local wrestling circuit. One clipping describes how Ricky set the state record for having the most bones broken in one match: four ribs, two teeth, and 'part of his leg.' He didn't mention this to any of the referees at the time, because he didn't want to be disqualified – he wanted to win. Which he did.

I approach Ricky and set my goods directly on the table. I figure this is not a man with whom to skirt words.

"Mr. Ricky," I say, "I need you to stitch this poem on these panties."

He looks calmly up at me, and in a voice that rumbles like one of the rigs outside, says, "No."

"Please," I say. "No one else in town can."

"No," he says, and returns to his scarf, as though I have conveniently stopped existing.

"Kathryn sent me."

"Two hundred bucks," he says. "Ready in a week."

"I can't afford that!" I cry out.

"One-eighty," he says, "Ready in two weeks. One-fifty, ready in a month."

By now I do not know whether to be annoyed or afraid. "The most I can pay is fifty dollars, sir," I say. "I don't have much –"

Ricky breaks my sentence off like a cracker. "You ain't one of *them*, are you?" he growls.

I have no idea what this could mean. "No, sir," I say cautiously. "I'm sorry, but I'm late to take my – duck – to – the vet. Thanks for your help."

"One-forty," he calls, as I walk out. I don't care. His scarf didn't look so hot anyway.

Driving home I begin to feel as though all the seamstresses in town are conspiring against me, that no one really believes this poem and these panties were destined for one another. Perhaps they are right; perhaps I should write another, smaller poem or find another, larger pair of panties. But I don't want to call my friend just yet to admit defeat, nor do I want to take up needlework myself. In a flash of inspiration I think of those Korean immigrants who will write your whole name on one grain of rice, but I have never seen any of them in Mendenhall.

In frustration I call Kathryn at work. When she finally picks up she puts me immediately on hold. She likes to make me listen to the pre-recorded music, even if there's no customer currently at her desk.

"Fabrics," she says cheerily, after a few minutes.

"You know I hate that."

"Yep," she chirps, "What was on?"

"Manilow. Again. And John Tesh."

"Oh, that's not so bad."

"Ugly is in the eye of the beholder, too, you know," I say. "What's up?"

"I went to Gritty Ricky's. I don't think he liked me very much."

"Oh, I'm sorry, dear. I should have told you. Ricky doesn't like anyone."

"Then how does he keep his store alive? The place was deserted! I mean, except for me and his stupid scarf," I add.

"He does fine," says Kathryn. "You weren't there at the right time. Early in the morning he gets all the fishermen who are going out on the lake. They breakfast at Dan's and gas up at the Shell, then hit him for catawba worms and line and tackle."

"I see," I say. "I guess I just missed all the action."

"Not that you're the earliest of birds," she says. "*J'accuse.*"

I harrumph into the phone.

"Hey, I have to go," says Kathryn. "Manager's here. Come by my place after I get off work. We'll drink beers and watch spy movies. It'll be fun."

"You sure know how to make a body feel better."

"If you're not careful I'll start charging you," she says. "In poems."

I have not actually written Kathryn any poems, for which I feel slightly guilty. She has given me two already, one she wrote when I fell asleep at her writing desk, and then a sestina she wrote after our first date, using end words from the Mondrian: *line*, *color*, *solid*, and so forth. The language was simple but the poem was stunning. She told me the first draft included the word *shark*, but as I have seen no manuscripts I am not sure I believe her.

That night we are watching *Spy Game*, with Robert Redford and Brad Pitt. I have always had a thing for

Robert Redford, nor have I ever been ashamed to admit it. The man is *magnificent*. Sometimes I imagine myself winning one of those "Ask Any Celebrity a Question" contests you see in the junk mail in the Sunday papers, and while of course I know who I would choose I always go back and forth as to what I would ask him. Some days I really want to know what it was like to kiss Mia Farrow and still be only acting, which is maybe most days, and then others I want to know why he never pushed to be James Bond. If his hair were a little darker he would be a shoe-in, I think. Usually Kathryn agrees with me, though she wants to know why Mel Gibson was never Bond either: the nationality issue aside, the man was born in a tuxedo, and plus, he has the best-looking five o'clock shadow in Hollywood. So she says. I wouldn't know.

Kathryn's calico comes padding up to us as we lie on the couch, and decides it wants to watch Robert too.

"See?" I say. "It spans even species."

Under the blanket Kathryn elbows me to be quiet. She is not one of those Nazis who forbids all conversation during a movie, but she is not far off. Talking during transitions is fine, and commenting on literary things is okay too, but if someone in the movie is speaking or looks like they are about to then you better finish your sentence quick or else suffer the consequences. I prefer to think of her as a movie-Nazi sympathizer.

"Beer?" I say, and stand. She nods without taking her eyes off what Robert is saying.

In the kitchen I see the dishes have won yet another battle in the war. I take the sponge and fill up the sink and wash a few, looking out into the backyard, wondering idly how things came to this: how one friend led to another, how a thing, in general, can lead to another. How something as simple as wanting a poem stitched on another person's undergarments can lead to a few more poems and a few other undergarments. There was a writer, once, I can never remember who, that had this idea of time not as a line or a circle but as a spiral: though he never said so, I'm pretty sure he thought of this while standing over the toilet, watching the way the water swirled around and around before disappearing. Which *can* be pretty interesting to watch, and to think about, if you let it.

"Where's the beer, dear?" Kathryn calls. "With apologies for the rhyme – you know I can do better."

I leave the sponge there, bobbing like a little rubber ducky in its little soapy ocean, and carry two beers back into the living room where Kathryn is waiting for me. When I enter she smiles. I set the bottles down on the table and pop them open with my new opener, the one from the aquarium that is shaped like a shark. Crawling back underneath the blanket, I find her hand just where I left it.

On screen Robert is on the phone with Brad Pitt, telling him not to stay in Beirut, but I have missed why this is the case. Which I don't mind so much, I guess. Some days, I imagine myself standing there in front of him, all the cameras trained and all the lights flashing, and then, just as I am about to speak, I forget my question.

The Center of the Universe

by Ryan Roark

Throughout my childhood, I thought of my mother as the beautiful, tragic victim of a disease beyond her control, a Dido, an Antigone, a Persephone – only more "nervous." My father was a willing martyr because of his overwhelming love for this girl who never quite managed to mature into a woman.

When they married, she was twenty-two and he over twelve years her senior. Sometimes I thought of him as the lucky suitor. My mother was in fact beautiful and had already had several boyfriends and two proposals. One of her then-suitors is now a famous country singer, and I didn't find out until quite recently that he wasn't famous at the time. He also abused her and she didn't leave him, but the story goes that my father was prompted to propose only three months after he started dating my mother because this singer said he was going to surprise everyone and marry her.

At other times, I thought of my mother as a strange choice for my father. Although I constantly heard her compared to Marilyn Monroe and him to Buddy Holly (I surmise from photos that this refers to a funny pair of glasses), he owned several live-music clubs and was well known around town (which was pretty small back then). To my mother, who frequented such establishments, he was a celebrity. He also had lots of girlfriends, including a couple who tried to commit suicide when they learned of his engagement. But for some reason he decided within those three months that he wanted to spend the rest of his life with my mother, who had seen so little of the world. She had never been on an airplane, never eaten broccoli, never been to a snake farm.

The proposal itself was romantic enough to fuel my notions for several years. He asked her to go to Cozumel with him. There, he proposed in a restaurant with one of those paper tablecloths you can write on. He wrote "I love you" and "Will you marry me?" in three different languages. She said yes and kept the tablecloth. This seemed beautiful to me for a long time, but now it seems slightly silly, because my mother doesn't and never did speak a word of any language other than English. It was heroic on his part, nonetheless.

They got married in the October after her college graduation, and I was born the following August. He had saved her from abusive parents and delivered her into a safe world entirely new to her. On the honeymoon, he found out she was insane, if that word really has any meaning. There were some wedding-ring-throwing incidents, but that only increased the romance and epic interest for me, once I had read *Tender Is the Night* and *Wide Sargasso Sea*.

When my parents married, my father was just starting to move away from the nightclub business and towards his present business, which is the one that made him money. Back then, he didn't make much, but he didn't have to work much, and so we were able to spend a lot of time together as a family in our small pseudo-bohemian house, where we lived until I was nearly five and which I recall as being vaguely donut-shaped. One year, mom said, we had to start going to the Laundromat because they couldn't afford to fix the washing machine. Of course, in the portrait she painted, she was all-patient and economizing, and it was very like something I'd seen in a movie, especially after my dad prevailed and turned his business into the leviathan it is now. Now I realize he had lost his illusions the first day she stood on the back porch screaming "fuck you" at the top of her lungs, or the day he was forced to leave me (an oblivious six months old) at a restaurant with his banker and his banker's wife because my mother threw a fit in the restaurant and ran down Main Street tearing her clothing off, jumping in front of cars, and eventually stabbing my father in the arm with a pair of scissors. The glamour of the nightclub business and the whole world they had known when dating was over. My father's business became a refuge, something to define his success and his happiness, and maybe the life he chose was more fulfilling than one he might have had with a sane wife. His marriage to such a woman would probably still have gone the unhappy way of most modern-day marriages. And after all, despite her emotional problems, my mother did love him very much, worshipped him – of that I am still convinced.

Even my mother's first stay in the mental hospital could be romanticized – she prevailed over her illness, declared that the other patients in the suicide ward were "completely crazy," and came back home. She was a good mother for several years after that, with relatively few lapses.

My father encouraged these fantasies of mine, and he had me convinced that they were still in love, even until I went to college. Soon after leaving home, though, I ceased to understand how that could be true. Once they got a divorce, after twenty years of marriage, he said they stayed together largely for logistical reasons, and particularly for my benefit. He insists this was the right thing to do. Now everything fits into place much more realistically – and heartbreakingly. I don't want to revise the tableau of my childhood, but it's impossible to preserve it with no regard for the present. It's impossible to suppress the anger I feel belatedly about my mother's behavior, anger I very rarely felt when I was living with her. It's so much easier to forget about my childhood, to lose memories – or to pretend it doesn't matter.

When I was in high school, I didn't dream at night. Sometimes I had nightmares, but I never remembered what they were about; I was just vaguely relieved to wake from them. Before that, I had dreams, but they almost inevitably involved my knowing they were dreams and telling the other characters in them that they were not real, that they were part of the dream, that I would wake up soon, although I couldn't control when that would happen.

Now I dream again from time to time, but usually what I'm left with in the morning is an image like something out of a manual for psychoanalysis of dreams. Last summer I had one that stuck with me; all I remember from it is one frame: a small bird sitting on top of a large egg. The image was too cute, like something on a birthday card I would display on my dresser. My father was so proud of this dream when I told him about it; he said, *it's an image of you: taking the weight of the world on your shoulders.* That's his favorite expression for what I do. I think it's pompous and suggests martyrdom, and I cringe when he says it.

Perhaps I did try to take on too much when I was little – after all, an only child is the center of her universe; she has no reference point besides herself. My parents never tire of telling me delightedly how selfish I was when I was little, and, much to my chagrin, they have the videotapes to prove it. In one of the family videos, starring me at age three, my father plays the role of a "friend."

Oh, Lucy, this is such a nice *toy. May I play with it?* He pets the toy. My face is darkening into various shades of gray, but I do not deign to say anything. I've already determined the fate of this toy. *What are you going to do now, Lucy?* Half the fun of the game was saying my name in sugary tones.

I'll BURN it!

He looks gleeful – not stopping here. *What if you were a child on the Titanic, and you had to share a lifeboat or DROWN?* (He was a member of the Titanic Historical Society; we had copies of the *Titanic Commutator* on the coffee table and posters of the ship on our walls. For his birthday one year, I drew a series of crayon pictures of it at a ninety-degree angle to the water, going down, as little stick girls with stick teddy bears watched on from the lifeboats.)

I'd DROWN!

But at this point I look gleeful too. I feel certain now, looking back, I was in on the joke, but my parents assure me we had to have cupcakes at my birthday party that year because I couldn't have borne the indignity of sharing a cake. By the time I started grade school, at the age of five, they had shamed me to the point that I smuggled my toys to school to give to my classmates. "Sharing" was synonymous with "good." But I hadn't stopped being the focal point in my own worldview, and perhaps that's why I thought I could take responsibility for other people – in particular, my mother. My father made a point of telling me all the time that nothing she did was my fault (although she made a point of telling me it was), and by sheer bombardment he had me nearly convinced. Nonetheless, I couldn't rid myself of the feeling that I could undo part of the damage, that if I blocked the door with a chair and stood there long enough, she wouldn't leave the house when she had a fit. Maybe I never really expected this to work, but taking action was the only way of bearing the fear of impending implosion. I was certain that, if she walked out that door in a rage, unspecified bad things would happen.

When I got older, I quit doing damage control and focused on preventing the damage from the get-go. By this time I had learned that when she did make it out of the house, she generally didn't make it out of the driveway or, if she did, she had nowhere to go. I had also learned that she usually ran out of steam fast; the kind of energy required for a fit cannot be sustained for more than a couple of hours. The real damage came from exposure: if more people witnessed her anger, then more people might think that she was crazy or worse, that she had a reason to be angry, that my father mistreated her (fortunately, no one could possibly believe that a child was mistreating her to such an extent – at least, I hoped not).

After she threatened suicide in front of one of my most innocent and conservative friends, while we were on vacation with her family, I decided that only my very closest friends would see my mother and only when necessary. This is not to say she would have an episode every time she saw one of them; she did go through long periods with none, but there was always the threat, the knowledge that the storm could come with absolutely no warning. Her anger was a time bomb, ticking in my ear even when I was eating lunch with her peacefully. I could ignore the tick most of the time, but not if there were other people around. The time bomb was sensitive to what was going on outside, too – the danger of explosion was often directly proportional to the need for calm, to the threat that it wouldn't be suppressed. When I was in high school, I had an interview for a very selective summer program. The interviewer wanted to have the interview at my house. My mother stayed in her bedroom the entire time, biting her fist until it bled, to keep from screaming out. This put a thin wall between my composedly answering nerve-wrackingly dogmatic questions from an interviewer who was scrutinizing every corner of the house and asking me critically about my private high school, and my mother's red face rocking to and fro in agony.

Perhaps the reason my father says I take the world on my shoulders – and the reason it bothers me so much – is that, when you're living in a continual crisis, it does begin to seem like all there is in the world, and that's an extremely arrogant viewpoint. Now I know there was nothing I could do when I was little to help my mother. But, on the other hand, I also know she wasn't lying when she said I was the reason she would leave or do harm to herself because, even more than I thought I was the center of the universe at age three, my mother has never been able to shake the suspicion that everything is about her. If I had boys over, she wanted to know if they said I had a young-looking mother. If I was worried about where I would go to college, she screamed she never had the opportunity to choose. If I did well in school, that was evidence she was a good mother. If I acted up, that was evidence she was the most put-upon woman on the planet. And if my father sided with me after she flew off the handle for a few hours, she was leaving.

I often think it would have been better if she had kept her word and left back then. Then again, I can't be sure that if she had, I wouldn't have imploded as I feared I would. I don't know. There's a lot to look back on and a lot of room for misplaced romanticizing and only one thing I'm sure of: when she finally did leave, it felt like the right thing.

Mostar Bridge, Summer 2005

by Heather Mcrobie

I. Law Of Averages

I did the maths. If you averaged out thirty five sample conversations that took place between the hours of 10pm and 2am, in the third room on the right, on the second floor, in the building opposite the library, back in Oxford, in the months that followed the miscarriage, you would find that your sum would be:

"Are you sure it doesn't hurt?"
"Please stop asking."
[Soft noises]
"What's the matter now?"
"I can't relax. You never say when it hurts."
"It doesn't hurt."
"Can we shift a bit? My arms are aching."
[Soft noises]

"*What*, David?"
"I'm sorry. I'm worried."
"Don't be worried. Ssh."
[Soft noises]
"I...can't stop thinking about it. Can we stop?"
"Oh, for fuck's sakes."

[Noises from shifting bed-sheets, curtains being drawn or otherwise adjusted, the setting of the next day's alarm on a mobile phone, fetching glasses of water.]

"Are you asleep?"

"Yes, I'm asleep David."
"Very funny."
"Go to sleep."
[Soft noises]

"You're not asleep. You're upset with me."
"I'm fucking asleep David. Leave me alone."
"It hurt you, didn't it?"
[Noises: pulling away, the hugging of bed-sheets, hands on themselves – a shift to a chair? – more glasses of water.]

And thirty-five sample nights will yield again for us the distance: of the room, on the second floor, opposite the library: the distance between David's hair uncombed and David's hair unstroked, between the high window where they lean out to smoke and the high window that is watching, between what counts as 'late' to them and what counts again as 'early', between David's shorts and T-shirt pulled back on or entering again the market-place of collective mess: waiting books, used coffee cups, potentialities of papers, gaping shoes and patient satchels.

"I wish you'd bloody tell me when it hurt."
[Softer noises, muffled by pillows]

II. Interactive Element

Please write in a legible hand, in either *blue* or *black* ink

SECTION A: IN THE HOSPITAL

You *may* tick more than one box

1. Were the other patients

Rosy-cheeked locals (who wished her well) ☐
U.N soldiers (older than she was) ☐
Bosnian soldiers (younger than she was) ☐
Prickled things whereupon to pin the edges of breathing-mask nightmares ☐
A soft, sweet blur of sounds, possibilities ☐

2. Did the doctor

Speak English learnt from 'Friends' episodes ☐
Tell a story about his daughter ☐
Tell a story about his wife ☐
Make her heart beat faster all evening ☐
Make her feel sick with his fingernails ☐

3. If he made her heart beat faster, was it

Because he reminded her of a film star ☐
Because his hands were cold ☐
Because his hands were an unexpected warmth that gave her a new sense of her own coolness ☐
Because he got the nurse to give her a few adrenalin shots ☐
Because he made her laugh so hard that he really, actually, genuinely, had to re-do two of her stitches ☐

SECTION B: CONVERSATIONS

You may tick only one box for each question

1. Who, of the following, said to her: "I'd like you to run through the story again, of why you jumped off the Mostar bridge"

David, her boyfriend ☐
The nurse ☐

The hospital psychiatrist ☐
The hotel manager ☐
The local journalist, picking at a scab ☐

2. Who, of the following, said to her softly: "Come on angel, you can tell me. I promise I won't be cross. Why did you do it? *If you knew*, I mean. Why did you do it if you knew?"

David, her boyfriend ☐
The nurse ☐
The hospital psychiatrist ☐
The hotel manager ☐
The local journalist, flicking a cigarette butt ☐

3. Who, of the following, was the only one to believe her midnight explanation:

"I watched the boys and men doing it all morning
And nobody said it would hurt.
The man in the mosque said that it was tradition,
That the local boys do it
To prove they're in love.
I thought that David could watch me and laugh,
Or take my picture or something.
I did it because I was so happy.
Yes, I know it sounds stupid now.
But it was so sunny, and we were so happy,
It looked like a fun thing to do."

David, her boyfriend ☐
The nurse ☐
The hospital psychiatrist ☐
The hotel manager ☐
The local journalist, shifting from foot to foot ☐

4. Who, of the following, did she *not* expect to question her honesty with the intrusive sentence: "If you didn't know that you were pregnant, why did you think you hadn't had your period for almost, what, two months?"

David, her boyfriend	☐
The nurse	☐
The hospital psychiatrist	☐
The hotel manager	☐
The local journalist, leafing through his local-journalist notebook	☐

SECTION C: EXCHANGES

1. Please draw a line between all the names in the list according to the secret glances, the embarrassed, silent, eyelash-based exchanges, or else the imperceptible leanings in hotel lifts, or huddled, lingering sharings of cigarette lighters, or shy offers to fetch some quote-unquote "coffee", from the hospital's only vending-machine, that were exchanged in Mostar, Bosnia, in the summer of 2005.

[Your answer *may* include: who dreamt of who, not in masturbation, but in the sense of kissing a pillow, or stroking your forehead and dreaming the touching hand is somebody else's]

The girl	David
The nurse	The doctor
The man in the mosque	The second-year Oxford tutor
The Austrian tourist	The girl in the Turkish café that overlooked the Mostar Bridge

2. Please draw a line between all those who had secret conversations, whispered, mumbled, in corridors, in offices, by her own hospital bed, while she was sleeping, late at night, early morning, chewing on a plastic cup, smoking a cigarette, caffeine-fiddling with their car-keys, or else springing back from the automatic doors as they sprang back from him in turn, in Mostar, Bosnia, in the summer of 2005, all on the topic of: "Do you really believe she didn't know she was pregnant, when she jumped off the Mostar Bridge?"

The girl	David
The nurse	The doctor
The man in the mosque	The second-year Oxford tutor
The Austrian tourist	The girl in the Turkish café that overlooked the Mostar Bridge

END OF TEST. PLEASE PUT DOWN YOUR PENS.

III. Spectator Sport

1.58pm
and now she's stretching – or is she already, no, just stretching, two boys over the side already you'll notice and it's going to have to be second place for the fat one with the young girl's breasts – oh! and is she going for it, already – no, just looking are we love – oh! well! we have a surprise entrance on the left – I'm told that he's one of the oldest men in Mostar – who last jumped off here before proposing to his wife – something like forty-five years ago, wasn't it – ooh, good impact – and he al-

ways said – even after they blew the original bridge up, in 1993 – that he'd do it one more time for her – before he died – isn't it grand they reopened the bridge on time – yes, I think, I *think* that that's his son handing his old man a towel – paramedics in place – isn't that lovely – the whole family – but hang on a minute! Hang! A! Bout! is she – no. oh! taking off the cardigan! interesting choice. keeping the blue dress on though. lovely.

1.59pm
more stretching – bit shaky with the old toe-touching – you sort of, er, you sort of get the feeling that she's still not sure, or that she might even be about to give up and – no, no, I'm wrong, I'm wrong! the girl from Oxford is, is jumping – jumping off the Mostar Bridge – on this beautiful day – the summer dress – it's like – a flower – opening – will she – yes, there – just, there – right in the centre – and I think that's clapping that you can hear – and her boyfriend, David – up there, watching – not the traditional way around, of course – but still, he's there, in the centre – watching her – is he filming? he's waving – and isn't he a good-looking young man, folks – *what a smile* – who wouldn't jump off there for him, eh? – and now he's coming down – to put his arms around her – I bet he won't – forget today – in a hurry – I bet he won't – ever forget – that sight.

The Changing Room

by Christopher Morley

Every Tuesday the school would take us to the dingy eight-lane swimming pool in Entcombe. We'd swim up and down, lumped with those dirty polystyrene floats that looked as if they'd been kicking about on a building site for a year or so before being mauled by dogs. We clasped them loathingly in our hands, we pinioned them clumsily between our feet, we had them crammed unsympathetically under our stomachs. Nobody enjoyed it. If they did then they kept quiet about it for fear of dead-legs, dead-shoulders, kidney punches, that sort of thing. I hated school swimming lessons in particular. I hated them because we weren't allowed to wear swim shorts, only trunks. I hated them because I didn't see the point of getting on a coach, driving ten miles to Entcombe – the arsehole of the universe – getting changed into our ridiculous trunks, being made to walk through that vat of disgusting foot-wash, having the instructors read out the safety rules as if they were reading us all our rights, and all for only an hour's swim. It sounds stupid, but I also hated those swimming sessions because I'd just started slicking my hair into a quiff. It would've been fine if I was able to re-do it afterwards, but caring about your appearance was another dead-leg offence, so I couldn't. Most of all though I hated swimming because the chemicals they used in that pool were caustic. They made my eyes sting and my lower legs itch like hell. If we'd lived in the US, I would've sued somebody's ass. But we didn't. We lived in Devon. And besides, I was only twelve.

It was the last week of term. The final swimming session. To mark the occasion, our instructors, a gangly-looking pervert of a man called Anthony, with lank blonde hair and a weasely face, and Harriet, an overweight, middle-aged woman with yellow toenails and podgy underarms, had promised us half an hour's free-time at the end. Usually we were lucky to get ten minutes. Like trained sea-lions, we swam lengths and retrieved the colourful hoops, bricks and other pointless items from the bottom of the pool for the first half hour. I never did understand it. Did they honestly think that painting the hoops pretty colours would take the edge off the ordeal? Anyhow, when they finally released us, I swam straight to the deep-end, turned over onto my back and let myself float. I enjoyed floating like this, just bobbing up and down gently and feeling weightless.

Staring up at the panelled ceiling, with its confusion of stains and shadows, I thought about how much better the pool that me and my father used to go to was. How much more fun. How we used to go down the tube slides together. Sometimes I'd go first and stop myself halfway down so I could ambush him. The attendants didn't like it, but that just made it more fun; no colourful hoops for us. And how, when I learned how to do front-crawl properly, we used to race each other from one end of that pool to the other, shattering the reflection of the glass dome ceiling as we went.

He'd explained to me many times why we'd had to move. It was his job. The company he worked for had offered him a promotion if he moved to the Exeter office. Simple as that. I just didn't buy it though. I was smart for a boy of twelve – I knew I was – and I'd seen no evidence of a promotion. We'd moved into a non-descript, semi-detached house that was so similar to the one we'd lived in before that it was as if we'd stayed put and allowed the counties to re-shuffle themselves. The green Renault had moved with us. No new car. My dad wore the same tired old suits when he set off in the morning and the same tired old expression when he returned at night. He did the same hours on the same days, and so little was ever said about his new role that I felt as if I shouldn't mention it. My mother had no new clothes or jewellery to speak of and we'd had no holiday that year. Don't get me wrong, we weren't hard up. My father's job had always paid well enough and me and my mother never wanted for anything. Either way, to me it was clear. We hadn't moved to a new and better life at all. We'd moved away from an old and untenable one. My parents had been at each other's throat for quite some time before the move, and there were obviously too many skeletons back in Nottingham. I guess moving away might have been their drastic equivalent of 'going on holiday to sort things out' or any of the other short-sighted measures that couples take when their relationship has really run its course.

As I floated around in my own little prison, wondering how I felt about the whole situation, about being uprooted, being kept in the dark, about being lied to, I felt a sudden impact around my waist. The breath in my lungs was replaced by chlorinated water and my eyes, wrenched from the despair of the roof, were submerged and stinging. Looking down through the haze of bubbles, I could make out a pair of arms wrapped tightly around me. I immediately recognised the bulging forearms of Terry Stubbs. He was one of those unnaturally massive school kids who are good at sports because of their size, the ones who fade into mediocrity after a few years, when everybody else catches up physically. Even through my breathless panic, I could picture his ugly face and that smug expression that he always wore. It was the earliest occasion I can remember when I thought I was going to die.

He held me down, as I wriggled like a bait-worm, my lungs screaming for air, my arms thrashing about pathetically. It wasn't a joke. It was an assault. It was cruel. If it had been a joke, as he later insisted to the police it was, he would have released me quick. But he didn't. Instead, I felt his stomach deflate as he calmly exhaled and allowed his dead-weight to drag us both to the bottom of the pool. No, he was trying to scare the shit out of me, and he was succeeding, holding me firmly enough that I hadn't a hope of escaping. Actually that's not true. He held me just loosely enough that I thought I might have a hope of struggling free, when really I didn't. He'd wanted to see me struggle. But mostly, he'd wanted to see me fail.

As I felt myself beginning to pass from consciousness, he finally let go. I broke the surface of the pool shocked and gasping, my stomach and lungs full of that putrid water. My legs itching overtime. Already my head was full of thoughts; dangerous, vengeful thoughts. I could hear him laughing as I hauled myself up onto the poolside, still choking up water.

Terry Stubbs screamed and held his hands up to his face. We were in the changing room. Most of us were still draped in our towels, hair ruffled, grey plastic storage containers, in which we stashed our belongings while we swam, arrayed on the benches in front of us. He continued screaming hysterically and within seconds a frenzy of semi-naked school boys had formed around him.

The razor blade jutted out of his right eyeball like a key from a lock. Looking back I wish I could've turned it. The blood was gushing out in weak pulses, cascading down his pale cheeks and finally decanting from the end of his chin. It exploded into hypnotic spirals on the thin film of water above the mustard tiles, before reforming into rivulets and trickling into a drain. To be honest, I don't think anybody else saw it like I did.

He appeared rooted to the floor with shock. His hands had now left his face, hovering a centimetre or two away as if he feared to touch his own skin; fingers splayed and looking like they'd seized up, palms basted in blood. He looked like he'd gone into some kind of a catatonic stupor, as if his head was a crystal ball and he was some kind of mystic raving hideous portents to a distraught crowd. You probably won't believe me if I say that the whole thing was an accident. But it was. That didn't stop me enjoying it though.

I'd left the pool-side, still choking as Terry Stubbs' penetrating laughter raped my ears, and waded back through the tepid foot-wash into the changing room. It was empty and cold. Still shaken and shivering slightly, I slid behind the staff counter where all of our belongings were stashed neatly on a large wooden shelving unit pushed clumsily back against the wall. Somebody was supposed to be minding them, but there was nobody to be seen.

I still had no idea what I was planning to do, how exactly I was planning to get my revenge. All I knew was that he had to pay. I considered taking his things and dumping them all in the toilets or the bin or just all over the floor with its carpet of toenails and pubic hair. No, not enough. I scanned across the containers. All the contents were similar, the same navy blue sweatshirts with the garish school logo emblazoned across the front in bright yellow print. The same characterless grey trousers and creased white shirts. Bollocks! There was nothing to distinguish one box from another without rooting through all the pockets and checking the names in the school diaries. That would take too long. I paused, casting my mind back to the moment when I'd suddenly found myself wrenched from reality and struggling for air; when my eyes had fallen on those loathsome forearms.

That was it! 25. It was so simple. Written in permanent marker on his wristband, the number 25. Everybody had one to identify their own belongings. I looked to my own wrist as if to confirm the system. I was number 19. A sudden wave of excitement passed through me. Looking along to the end of the second shelf I could now see Terry Stubbs' storage container. The number 25 was daubed messily onto the scratched grey surface in red. The sleeve of his sweater hung over the edge, obscuring the top half of the 5 like an obsequious tentacle trying to protect its master. It had failed. Reaching up, I dragged the container to the edge of the shelf and brought it down onto the wooden stool where an attendant should have been sat. Here was the first conspirator. Still unsure what exactly my next move would be, I paused again, my eyes scouring the room for inspiration.

The razor blade was wedged into a plastic grate capping one of the changing room drains. Perfect! Making sure Stubbs' container was safely balanced on top of the stool, I picked up his towel, walked out from behind the staff counter and headed towards the mirrors on the opposite wall. These were the mirrors I would've used to re-style my hair, if it hadn't been for the likes of Stubbs. Approaching, I hardly recognised my own reflection. My face was pale, my skin still slick with water, my hair swept back like some kind of nineteen-fifties gangster. *Jamie Kray*. Had quite a ring to it. My muscles, tense with cold, made me look powerful and athletic. I remember thinking how such a look might grow on me in time.

The drain was immediately below the end mirror. I stooped down, my swimming trunks stretching taut and crushing my testicles even more than usual. My right hand gloved protectively in Stubbs' towel – I didn't want to go cutting myself – and my left holding the excess out of the way, I reached forward and took hold of the end of the razor. From the look of it, it had been lost rather than discarded, sharp and rust-free as it was. It was also firmly wedged and, as I struggled to wriggle it loose, the whole grate came away. Thankfully, this just made it easier to free the blade and, having done so, I replaced the grate and stamped it back into position. I side-footed back behind the counter; I didn't like the feeling of my entire sole patting on that filthy floor. It was 'other people' filthy. Then I stared down at the crumpled uniform before me. Decision time.

It's funny, now, to think of people who've had really serious decisions to make. Decisions with far-reaching consequences. Decisions such as whether or not to drop an atomic bomb, whether or not to invent one in the first place. Decisions on whether to go to war, whether to execute, assassinate, whether to murder. In my twelve year-old brain, the decision before me, the decision about how to get even with Terry Stubbs from Sutton High School class 3K was just as crucial.

Moments later and the decision was made. It was base and it was crude, but I was going to drop the bomb. I was going to score open the crotch in his trousers! This was virtually the end of the world for any schoolboy. Yes, I'd score it nice and finely right up along the arse-crack, leaving a few strands to keep the gash together temporarily. Then, as soon as he bent over to tie his shoe laces or pick something up: *riiiiiiiiip!* As I stood there, unable to prevent the blossoming of a rictus, I could see it. The painful embarrassment on his big repulsive face, the laughter. I could hear the gossip, the story being told again and again for the rest of our time at school, being immortalised in the final year-book! I could think of no better punishment. It was perfect.

But it was not to be. At that moment, a shrill blast tore its way fatefully through my vision. It was the whistle that signalled the end of the session. Conspirator number two. My time was up. I hastily bundled Stubbs' towel into his container and crammed it back into position on the shelf. Then I made my way quickly back out of the changing room to the showers.

So I'd forgotten it then. Left it speared into the towel when the attendant's whistle had arrested my hell-bent brain. Oops. Then he had slipped the thing neatly into his own eyeball. Case closed.

After the initial excitement, during which a number of other boys fainted, a number of girls intruded to see what all the screaming was about, and the various attendants and teachers had squawked around like headless chickens, Stubbs passed out on the floor with shock. He was taken to hospital in an ambulance. Except for me, nobody had the first idea what'd happened. It wasn't quite what I'd intended, of course, but it'd do. That same afternoon a full police investigation started up. After they'd operated to remove his eyeball, a humbler, all together nicer Terry Stubbs told the police that I was to blame. He told them that I was trying to get even with him after he'd played a joke on me. What a load of crap! A couple of the other boys mentioned that they thought they'd seen me leave the pool early as well, but it was all still very hazy – especially for Captain Stubbs, I'd imagine.

I was called in for an official police interview the next day, the same as everybody else who'd been in the changing room. I was definitely prime suspect though. I could tell. Whenever police turn up a blank they have to cling to anything, any little shred of evidence, no matter how weak; even I knew that. Stubbs' schoolboy finger-pointing and the fact that two other boys thought they might possibly, maybe, perhaps have seen me leave the pool early at some point was shred enough. But I knew I was safe. I knew I was safe because it was a genuine accident. If I'd actually meant to stab the fucker in the face with a razor blade, then I might have found it harder to lie to the police.

But I hadn't.

So I didn't.

"Okay Jamie, can you tell us what happened in the swimming pool yesterday, when Terry Stubbs had his accident? Talk me through from when you arrived on the coach."

I remember thinking the policewoman was pretty. She was trim and blonde, with flawlessly tanned skin, like the women on the magazines my mother used to read and my father used to hide under his mattress. But she was a little bit older, could've been a mother herself, I guess. Her eyes were kind and she took her hat off when she sat down to speak to me. The other one just lurked around in the shadows at the back of the room. I never even saw his face. My father was sat next to me. His hands were clasped together on the table in front of him, his head lowered and turned towards mine slightly. His expression was that same façade of serenity that he'd mastered so well and his right thumb passed rhythmically up and down the length of the left, like a silent metronome. I slid into that rhythm, using it to temper my speech.

"We always go to the pool on Tuesday, but this was the last time this term because next week's the summer holidays," nice and natural, nice and puerile. "Then we did some lengths and some life-saving."

"Do you like doing life-saving Jamie?" She smiled sweetly at me as she finished speaking. Now I could see her game. Even at twelve, I could see that she was trying to win me into her confidence, this pretty, motherly figure. She wanted my lips nice and loose. If I'd been a bit older she'd probably have worn a low-cut top, so she could lean across the table at me and crush her tits together into an arse and make me suddenly confess everything. I dropped my eyes over to the subtle whirring of the dictaphone on the edge of the table. I decided that when I looked back up I wouldn't see a pretty lady anymore. I decided I would see something foul. I've always been able to do that. To look at something and see it differently, the way I want. Sometimes it can be hard to do, particularly as I've gotten older. Sometimes, though, it just happens.

"Jamie?" It was my father's voice. "Answer the lady's question," he urged, firm and gentle.

He was right. I was taking too long. I was making myself stand out, making myself look guilty.

"Sorry," I said, looking up at the crusty skin that was peeling away like strips of bark below her sickly yellow eyes.

"That's okay," she replied, the edges of her teeth stained black as if she'd been sucking on a lump of coal. "Do you?"

"Yes, I quite like life-saving." Her breath was stale and repulsive, but I wouldn't let on that I could smell it, that it was wafting into my face like sonic-booms of cow-fart. That would be rude and I had to protect her. I had to be the one in charge here. "I'd like to be able to help somebody if they couldn't swim. Sometimes we have to get colourful hoops off the bottom of the pool as well and I quite like that too."

I noticed a look of surprise flicker across my father's face. He could smell something too, but for him it was plain old rat. He knew me too well. I couldn't stop now though. If he suspected anything and wanted answers, I'd have much preferred to confide 'the accident' in him later than admit 'the crime' right then and there.

"Good for you," the policewoman said. I noticed her name on the interview sheet in front of her. Officer Debby Conran. "So what happened after you did life-saving?"

"We had free time," I replied. "We had longer than most weeks because it's the end of term."

"So what did you do with *your* free time, Jamie?"

Now she was getting down to business. What *do* I do in my free time? Ooh, steal, fight, start fires, stab people in the face. I've thought about murder but I might hold fire on that one for a while, after all I need something to fall back on, don't I?

"I swam over to the deep end and floated around a bit."

"Did you play with any of your school friends?"

"No, I like…" I stopped myself short. I couldn't very well have told her that I was a loner who liked floating motionless on his back, staring up at the ceiling and worrying about home-life. No, that was the sort of thing unstable people that stabbed each other in the face did. It was, as I was well aware, a little strange.

"I like practicing life-saving and diving to the bottom and things."

Officer Conran, her hair crawling like an insect nest, the occasional beetle dropping onto the table and scuttling off the edge, shuffled the papers in front of her.

Thanks for the heads up. It was crunch-time.

"Did you see Terry Stubbs at all, Jamie? While you were practicing."

Good question. Clever. Did I see Terry Stubbs.

"Yes I saw him," I replied. "I don't really know Terry that well. Don't really talk to him at school." Then I added, "I've heard a lot of things about him though."

Her expression changed.

So did my father's.

Officer Conran's – still peeling away to the bone – looked decidedly more interested. My father's, which luckily the policewoman didn't notice, looked decidedly more surprised. He knew my history with Terry Stubbs all too well. I knew Terry well. I knew him well because he used to bully me, still did sometimes. But then he bullied a lot of people. It was all okay though. I felt confident that this wouldn't leave a hole in my story if she cared to play sleuth. I'd begged my parents not to mention the bullying to the school, explaining to them that it would just make it worse and did they want to make my life even harder and so on. Begrudgingly they'd agreed. So none of the teachers knew there was a problem between us, and Officer Conran could poke about all she wanted.

"What sort of things, Jamie?"

"I've heard that he can be quite mean."

"Mean?"

"Yeah, to other kids." Carefully does it Jamie. Discredit Terry, but don't give yourself motive.

"And what sort of things have you heard that he does to other children?" Without lifting her eyes from me, Debbie Conran took a sip of her coffee. She left most of her leprous lips on the rim, the steaming liquid filtering its way back out of the cribbage board of wood-worm holes on her neck and soaking into her blouse.

"He steals things off the other children," I said, "and pushes them around. Mostly girls. Then if they tell the teacher about him he always tells lies to get out of it." I paused for a moment, looking Officer Conran straight in the eyes. They were oozing something green at the corners. "That's just what I've heard though. I just try and keep away from people like that so that I don't make them steal *my* things."

She sat back in her chair.

"Terry Stubbs said that he dunked your head under the water yesterday. Is that true Jamie? Did he do that? Or did he just splash water at you or something?"

Very smart.

"I did feel somebody knock into me hard at one point," I replied, "but I didn't see who it was because there were lots of us playing around in the same area so we knock into each other all the time. And anyway I wouldn't care if anyone did push me under because I love the water and I love diving under."

I couldn't tell whether it was satisfaction or exasperation on Officer Conran's face as she leant back towards me. She pulled one of those faint smiles that can mean any one of a million different things.

"Did you leave the swimming pool at any point Jamie?" She hadn't any teeth left, only hellish pink gums.

"I went to the toilet," I replied. It was make or break. Calculated.

Like a bloodhound that's picked up a faint but unmistakeable scent, her entire peeling face seemed to sharpen. Her fingers, covered in a forest of thick black hair, stopped shuffling the papers and flattened onto the table. They were tarantulas threatening to pounce.

"Can you remember when you went to the toilet Jamie?"

"In free time," I said. "I always try to go before the whistle."

"The whistle?"

"Err, the pool attendants blow their whistles when it's time for the children to leave the pool," my father interjected rapidly, as if trying to speed the whole process up.

"Oh yes, of course," Officer Conran said, bringing her hollow eyes immediately back to mine. "Why do you try to go before the whistle, Jamie?"

"Because if I need to…" I looked around, feigning embarrassment. "If I need to…" now I glanced up at my father, as if for permission to proceed. He nodded gently. "If I need to poo," I half-whispered, "I like to go before everybody else is around, because some of them bang on the door and throw things over the top and shout things. Then I can't go properly and it hurts." I continued looking flustered.

Officer Conran nodded sympathetically, sighed and sat back up in her chair. Her threat was diminishing. The entire case rested on me implicating myself. No chance! No CCTV, no fingerprints, no DNA, no *real* eyewitnesses. She just couldn't prove that my actions were anything other than what I'd told her. Couldn't prove that the blade hadn't been in the crate already, getting mixed up in Stubbs' towel. *And* I was convincing. I knew I was. The skin on her face started to patch itself back up. A surgical needle and thread flitted its way around her lacerations at the whim of invisible hands. The insects fled *en masse* out of her hair, down her body and onto the floor, leaving her blonde again. Her lips were back.

"When you went to the toilet did you see anybody else?"

I thought for a moment. Genuinely. A dark thought gathered on one of my many mind-horizons. It was unstoppable. Come to think of it, I'd seen Anthony the gangly attendant leave the poolside shortly after the start of free-time. He often did this. From the smell of the guy, I'd say he popped outside – alone – for a cigarette or three whenever he thought he could get away with it. Yes. I'd seen Anthony on my way for a shit hadn't I. Gently does it.

"I think I saw one of the attendants."

"Really?" A look of obvious surprise crossed the policewoman's face. The man in the background shifted.

"I think so. I think it was Anthony, just outside the changing rooms. He must've been cleaning or something."

"Are you sure, Jamie?"

"Pretty sure, yes."

And that was all it took. A background check on swimming instructor Anthony Harding revealed that he'd been charged with assaulting three young boys over the course of as many years, indecent exposure to a boy of nine and the attempted abduction of a six year-old girl. He'd never been successfully convicted and after each incident he'd managed to disappear and re-emerge far from controversy, in the company of children. Of course, by this time, he was nowhere to be found.

Just like that, I was old news. Free to enjoy the summer holidays. Innocent. Just like that, poor old Captain Stubbs was yesterday's headline and it was Officer Conran and company who were in the dock. How could this have happened? How could Harding have slipped through the net? What was being done to apprehend him? Were they always this incompetent? The media had a field day.

As for me, my father never once questioned what I'd told the police. Never asked me what had really happened that day in the changing room. Never asked me to explain. It was obvious that he suspected something. I could see it in his face. But it seemed as if he couldn't quite put his finger on it. Either that or he didn't want too. In fact, it was almost two months later, as we waded into the shallow end of the old fun pool in Nottingham together – my thirteenth birthday treat – that he stopped suddenly and lowered both hands gently onto my shoulders. Pulling me around to face him, he launched straight into a speech about loving me and always being there for me and about how I could talk to him about anything. *Anything*.

I knew exactly what he meant. Without flinching I told him that I felt sorry for Terry losing his eye and having to wear a patch, and that it upset me to talk about it, especially on my birthday. He held my gaze momentarily, then just turned away and nodded, the way he does. Anyway, I splashed him with water to break the awkward silence. He splashed me back laughing, and without another word we dived in and raced to the other end of the pool. It was just like old times – I won, of course, even at thirteen. But I'm fairly certain he let me have that one.

You know, I often wonder why I didn't really feel bad about what happened in the changing room that day. No remorse. No guilt for lying to the police, or my father. In fact, would you believe me if I told you that it was the most enjoyable school swimming lesson ever?

No colourful hoops for me.

When Lunch Becomes Dinner

by Simon Pitt

For a long time now, Trent had been studying the work of philosopher and all round clever egg Dr Hubert Cupboard. Dr Cupboard's first major work[1] was, unfortunately, out of print. As were all of his other major works, something they had in common with his non-major works (in addition to having "Dr Hubert Cupboard" written on the front). In actual fact, it would be fair to say that every single one of Dr Hubert Cupboard's works, irrespective of magnitude, was out of print.

This in itself was not surprising. It was said that even Dr Cupboard's most famous work[2] had only been read eight times. And Trent had read it twice. He considered reading it again as he padded downstairs to the kitchen.

While he pondered idly what to have for breakfast, he tried to remember which of Dr Cupboard's books contained the chapter on contemplation[3]. It wasn't a chapter that he'd read much before, and he thought maybe he'd spend the morning reading that. Reading it would take maybe until about 11.30 – say 11.45 to be safe. That would give him time to go and meet Annette for coffee. Annette liked coffee. Trent liked Annette. He wasn't sure if that, therefore, led to the conclusion that Trent liked coffee, that Annette liked Trent or that

---

1 Dr Hubert Cupboard, *Initiating Thought in a Coexistent Manner* (Cambridge: Cambridge University Press, 1978)

2 Dr Hubert Cupboard, *Towards an Attitude of Rectitude* (Oxford: Oxford University Press, 1984)

3 Dr Hubert Cupboard, *Assessing Certitude*, (London: Routledge, Keegan and Paul, 1981) Chapter 6 "A contemplative consideration" pp 87 – 112

Socrates was a man, since he hadn't read Dr Cupboard's essay on deductive reasoning[4], but whichever was true, it meant that Trent spent longer than he would have otherwise in Starbucks.

It would be a lot easier, Trent thought as he took a bite out of loaf of bread, if he had studied the work of someone less... out of print. One of the biggest problems with Dr Cupboard was finding anything he'd actually written. The man's words had a remarkable ability to disappear. Strangely, there was a noticeable inverse proportion between the words 'by Dr Hubert Cupboard' on the front of the book and its sales figures.

Trent took another bite from the loaf of bread, and then wrapped it in a paper bag. The rest of the loaf, he thought, popping the package into his battered, brown leather suitcase, he'd save for lunch.

He hurried upstairs and performed the mandatory morning activities: brushing his teeth, hair and the crumbs off his jacket as appropriate; washing his hands, face and anything else that seemed to need washing. Ablutions completed, he tied his tie and left his house.

The nearest copy of *Assessing Certitude*, which contained the chapter on contemplation that Trent planned to read, was in the British Library, and could not be taken out of the reading room. Trent entered the Library, and wrote numbers down on the bits of papers that needed numbers written down on them so that Dr Cupboard's work would be produced. He signed the pieces of paper that the man with a lopsided jacket handed to him, until the man told him to stop. He went and sat in a chair for the estimated fetching time of 30 – 40 minutes.

When the book arrived he took it back to a desk, and began to paw over it. "When one ponders the act of con-

---

4 Dr Hubert Cupboard, "A Reconsideration of Aristotelian Logic: Deducing from Primary Principles", in *Intelligence Today*, Vol. 8, Issue 9, June 1976

templation," Dr Cupboard's words flowed up into his eyes, "it is all-to-easy to become fixated by the circularity of the self-reflexive act. Indeed, this common trap has been fallen into by Mr Lock (Lock, 1972) and Ms Appleton (Appleton, 1978) both of whom are respected thinkers in their fields."[5]

Trent lapped up Dr Cupboard's words. The man was, most certainly, a genius. Only a genius, after all, could write, "the act of considering contemplation is, primarily, a moral act; moral in Prof Heskin's most excellent definition (Heskin, 1976b)"[6]. Trent had never read Prof Heskin's most excellent definition. Nor had he read Lock, 1972, or Appleton, 1978, yet he knew for certain that both of the latter were respected thinkers in their fields who had, unfortunately, fallen into a common trap that Dr Cupboard had avoided.

Dr Cupboard avoided all sorts of traps that various other commentators fell into. Off the top of his head, Trent could think of four different traps that Dr Cupboard had adroitly sidestepped while other, less cautious, analysts had plunged headlong. Unfortunately, as foresighted as Dr Cupboard was in avoiding theoretical pitfalls, he hadn't been quite as good at avoiding literal ones, and had fallen down an open manhole to his death in May 1994[7]. Because of this, Trent would never be able to meet the great man himself. Secretly, he thought this was probably best. After all, the man could never have lived up to Trent's perception of him in reality. After all, someone who could write "the primary unit of perception, is, in many ways, less theoretical than experimental"[8] would always be a disappointment in reality.

---

5 Dr Hubert Cupboard, *Assessing Certitude*, (London: Routledge, Keegan and Paul, 1981) p 87

6 Ibid, p 94

7 *The Times*, Wednesday May 4th, 1994.

8 Dr Hubert Cupboard, "Parallel Perceptions: Experiencing Initial Realisations", in *Theoretical Review*, Vol. 28, Issue 12, March 1989

Trent left the reading room briefly. Before leaving he wrote the necessary details on a piece of paper to stop anybody taking away his copy of *Assessing Certitude*. Outside the library, he munched his way through half the loaf of bread. Loaves of bread always made him think of Dr Cupboard's 1986 Harvard lectures[9]. Trent hadn't actually been there, but he had found the copy of the transcriptions in a small second-hand bookshop in Portsmouth. That had been the highlight of his trip to Portsmouth really. He couldn't really remember much else about the holiday apart from that purchase.

Once he had ingested enough bread so that his stomach rumblings were quiet enough not to distract him from Dr Cupboard's words, Trent returned to the reading room. His book was where he'd left it, and Trent jumped back into it. He had to read over the last sentence a few times, to pick his way through Dr Cupboard's intricate syntax, but then he was off again.

At 11.35 he remembered that he was going to meet Annette for coffee. At 11.40 he remembered that he was going to meet her at 11.30. At 11.45 he realised he'd probably better run to get there. Hurriedly, he grabbed his coat, stopping only to fit the reserved slip back into *Assessing Certitude* at the page he was up to, and mentally making a note of the page he was on in case any careless librarians lost his place. Dr Cupboard's words, "In making this judgement there is a necessary element of ethical doubt, which cannot simply be ignored by reference to tangential application"[10] stared invitingly back at him, but they would have to wait for later.

---

9 "If we think of logic as like a loaf of freshly baked fine bread, then the type of reasoning that Dr Dagenham is exhibiting here would probably be a slice of blackened, rather burnt toast." From Hilary Fenton, Ed., *The Harvard Lectures Transcribed*, (Stanford: Stanford University Press, 1988)

He tucked the words away, and put the book on the edge of a seldom used table, so that it wouldn't get accidentally tampered with. Whether there would be anyone in the British Library reading room who would accidentally tamper with a copy of *Assessing Certitude* was very doubtful, but Trent didn't want to take that risk.

He hurried outside, retrieving his half eaten loaf of bread from the cloak room, and checked his watch. It was, he realised, going to be a taxi job to transport himself from the British Library to the Starbucks they had been planning to meet in. Either than or a run, and he was too full of dough to go running.

He telephoned for a taxi, repeatedly looking at his watch in an effort to make time go slower or the taxi arrive quicker. It didn't work. A few minutes later, the taxi pulled up, and Trent hurriedly climbed into the back, explaining to the driver where he wanted to go.

"Righto," the driver said, and hefted the steering wheel around, "shouldn't take too long, I know a shortcut there." Trent nodded relieved, leaning forwards, and staring eagerly ahead.

"Desperate for a coffee?" he asked Trent in conversation. "That happens to me sometimes."

"Going to meet a friend."

"Ah right," the taxi driver did some more unnecessarily vicious steering, "yeah, I have this friend, who I always meet in Costa. Nowhere else. He doesn't like it anywhere else. Says the coffee isn't as good. Me, I can't tell the difference." Trent agreed with him that all coffee tasted more or less the same. "Yeah, I mean, it's like with chess as well. To me, all the pieces look the same as well. Castle, rook, whatever. The same with a macchiato or a cappuccino."

"Yeah," Trent said, "you can drop me right here, that'll be fine." He knew very little about chess – except for how to castle. Dr Cupboard had used the idea as a metaphor

---

10 Dr Hubert Cupboard, *Assessing Certitude*, (London: Routledge, Keegan and Paul, 1981) p 102

in one chapter of his study on understanding[11].

"Sure thing boss, that's, what, £2.50?"

Trent gave him some coins and hopped out. The Starbucks was not large, but it had a table round the back that had soft chairs and a large plastic-leafed pot plant next to it. These two things in conjunction were about the pinnacle of a Starbucks' experience. He and Annette usually tried to get that table, often by resorting to leaving bags, shuffling nearer and nearer to the people currently sat there until they left, and other equally as unscrupulous means.

He found Annette sitting at their table in the back of Starbucks. The table was somewhat hidden beneath an army of mugs that sat on it[12]. From the look of it, Annette had worked her way down the Starbucks menu in alphabetical order. She was currently busily disposing of an Iced Caramel Macchiato Frappuccino.

"Oh, hello," she said. Her voice had a slight coldness to it that could only partly be blamed on the Iced Caramel Macchiato Frappuccino she was drinking. "Busy day?"

"Yeah, a bit," Trent said, sitting down, "can I get you a coffee?"

She looked through the cups that she had already collected, "I think I've probably got them all already," she said, "I've been waiting here twenty minutes." She paused, "again."

"Sorry," Trent mumbled.

"What was it this time? *Initiating Confluent Thinking*?[13]"

---

11 Dr Hubert Cupboard, *Deconstruction in Central Development* (London: Penguin, 1986) , Chapter 9 "Lateral Castling and Unimpeded Thought" pp 176 - 202

12 The sight reminded Trent of a diagram, featuring a number of upright towers on a three dimensional circular surface to illustrate the perpendicular flow of logical deductions. See Fig 14 in Dr Hubert Cupboard, *Initiating Thought in a Coexistent Manner* (Cambridge: Cambridge University Press, 1978) p 137

"*Intimating Confluent Thinking*," Trent corrected absently. "No, it was *Assessing Certitude*. You should read it, actually. It has a really good chapter on paradox entailments[14]."

"I'm not interested in paradox entailments, Trent," Annette said, "I did a degree in photography, I don't know what Bayesian probability[15] is, I can't even understand the title of most of Dr Cupboard's books."

"They're very good," Trent said. "The books I mean, not the titles. Although the titles are very good as well."

"With titles like *Assessing Certitude* they hardly leap off the shelves," Annette pointed out, "what's that statistic? Most of them have only been read four times?"

"Eight times," Trent corrected.

"Well still. Most people read the back of their cereals packets more often than that."

"Not me."

"You have toast for breakfast, Trent."

Trent sighed. "I just think that Dr Cupboard is a very underrated thinker. You know, he might be one of the most forthright and challenging intellectuals of our age."

"You've just read that off the front of one of his books," Annette said.

Trent shook his head. "No. No one has ever reviewed any of his works, so they haven't got any quotes to put on the front of them."

"Maybe there's a reason no one has ever reviewed them," Annette said.

Trent tried to raise an eyebrow quizzically, but suspected that he hadn't managed. "What's that?" he asked.

---

13 Dr Hubert Cupboard, *Intimating Confluent Thinking* (London: Penguin, 1982)

14 Dr Hubert Cupboard, *Intimating Confluent Thinking* (London: Penguin, 1982) Chapter 3, "Notions of formalised implication" pp 45 - 58

15 See Dr Hubert Cupboard, "Interpretation of Probability" in *Modern Thought Review*, Vol. 8 Issue 62 Summer 1984

"Because they're very boring. They're dull, dry and really, really incomprehensible. I mean, I know you quote that bit from the one about thinking in a something whatever about the reason for whatever[16], but I never understand it."

"That's not a reason to not study him though," Trent pointed out, "the man has a lot to say that is very relevant to the modern world."

"Well, perhaps, but, don't you think you're, maybe, taking your interest in him too far?"

"I don't think you ever can pursue intellectual aggrandisement too far," Trent said, "what do you mean, anyway?"

"Well, how long have we been meeting in this coffee shop?"

Trent made a side to side motion with his head as he counted. "Dunno," he totalled up, "quite a while."

"Okay, quite a while, that's good for a working figure. And, in that time, how many times have you been late because you've been reading one of Dr Hubert Cupboard's works on the profitability of fusing independent conveyance[17] or whatever."

Trent pondered, "A few," he admitted. "Okay, quite a few. Maybe even a lot."

Annette screwed up her nose in that way she did when she was trying to calculate the VAT on something. "Let me put it this way," she said, "if x is the number of times we've met in this coffee shop for coffee, and y is the number of times you've been late because you've

---

16 Dr Hubert Cupboard, *Initiating Thought in a Coexistent Manner* (Cambridge: Cambridge University Press, 1978), Trent often quoted: "The reasons for interpreting and attempting to redefine the central considerations, are, in many respects, bound up with their own interpolative deductions" p 186

17 Presumably this is a reference to Dr Hubert Cupboard, "On the practicality of focussing independent convergence" in *Intelligence Today*, Vol. 12, Issue 67, June 1981, Trent thought.

been reading Dr Hubert Cupboard's seminal work on blah, then, I put it to you, that x = y."

"I think that's a bit unfair," Trent said.

"Really?" Annette asked, "Okay, what about that time we went to Portsmouth for that weekend?" Trent thought back to it. "What do you remember about that week?"

Trent thought hard. He remembered purchasing a copy of Hilary Fenton, Ed., *The Harvard Lectures Transcribed*, (Stanford: Stanford University Press, 1988), for £4.50 in a small second-hand bookshop, but decided that would be the wrong answer. He remembered carefully rubbing the price out of the book with a soft rubber as well, but he suspected that wouldn't be the right answer either.

"I remember that time we went to the Portsdown Hill, and saw that view of Portsmouth from above," Trent said, remembering a picture of Portsmouth that was pinned to an obscure board at home. This, he thought, was probably the right answer. Annette sighed.

"We didn't go to Portsdown Hill. It rained for most of the week, so we just stayed in and bought postcards of aerial views from the newsagents over the road," she said. "Apart from that one time we went to that seedy little shop with the man wearing those funny trousers."

"Oh yeah," Trent said. "I remember that."

"No you don't," Annette sighed, "you remember buying that book with one of Cupboard's speeches in it."

Trent sighed. "Well," he said, but then couldn't think of any other words to follow it. "I don't like coffee you know," he added.

"What's that got to do with anything? I don't talk to you about Starbucks Caffè Americano (2006: £2.60 take away, £2.90 eat in), do I?"

"Maybe not, but we still come here."

"You don't have to drink coffee. You could have tea, or hot chocolate, or water, or a milkshake, or, quite revolutionary this, you could just have something to eat and go without a drink at all."

Dr Cupboard wouldn't have been proud of him for his argument Trent realised. "I don't see what you have against Dr Cupboard," he said, oozing reasonableness like jam from one of Starbuck's jam doughnuts (2006: £1.30 take away, £1.60 eat in). "Just because he is a deep thinker – anyone would think you have epistemophobia or something."

"What's epistemophobia?" Annette asked, suddenly sounding tired.

"Fear of knowledge."

"I'm not scared of knowledge. I'm not even scared of Dr Hubert Cupboard. It's just his books, with their titles, and all their footnotes and references and bibliographies – they're taking over your life."

"Dr Cupboard doesn't use footnotes, he usually the Harvard inline referencing system," Trent said before he could stop himself.

"See what I mean?" Annette said, "That's exactly my point."

"Maybe you're scared of footnotes," Trent suggested, "what would that be? Bibliographobia?"

"I'm not scared of footnotes. I'm scared that footnotes will take over you life. I'm scared that footnotes are your life. Footnotes and Dr Cupboard. I mean, I'm pretty sure you know more about Dr Cupboard than you know about me."

"Um." Trent said. The problem, he wanted to say, was that he'd read Dr Cupboard's autobiography three times now[18], and so knew the man quite well.

"You probably know more about Dr Cupboard than you know about yourself."

---

18 Dr Hubert Cupboard, *Coming out of the Cupboard*, (Oxford: Oxford University Press, 1990) whereas, as far as Trent knew, Annette had never written her autobiography. Or, if she had, it hadn't been published yet.

Trent pondered this for a few minutes. To be honest, he hadn't written his autobiography either. And, even if he had, he probably wouldn't read it three times.

"Well, anyway, I've got to go back to work now," Annette got to her feet, "Look, don't take this the wrong way. I'm not saying that you should stop reading Dr Cupboard entirely, but, I do think maybe you should do something else sometimes. I mean, occasionally have a day entirely free from Dr Cupboard's wisdom. There is such a thing as becoming obsessed."

She patted him on the shoulder, saying, "You free Thursday lunch time?" Trent nodded, since, on Thursday, he'd been planning to read Dr Hubert Cupboard, "Allowing Referent Allusiveness in Semantic Examinations" in *Philology Today*, Vol. 9, Issue 12, Summer 1984 pp 64 – 88[19]. In that article, Dr Hubert Cupboard had argued convincingly against the points raised by Mr Finnegan three months earlier. Referent allusiveness, a phrase that Mr Finnegan seemed to fundamentally misunderstand, was an essential part of semantic examination. "It seems now would be a most prodigious occasion", Dr Cupboard had written, "to observe that the importance Mr Finnegan attaches to referent allusiveness is indicative of a pervading misunderstanding of the term"[20].

Trent followed Annette out of Starbucks and made his way back to the British Library. This was a route that

---

19 Trent had read it three times before, and knew that it took him roughly an hour and a half to read. That would leave him plenty of time to get from the British Library to Starbucks, without having to catch a taxi and talk to the driver who was obsessed with draughts or whatever.

20 Dr Hubert Cupboard, "Allowing Referent Allusiveness in Semantic Examinations" in *Philology Today*, Vol. 9, Issue 12, Summer 1984 pp 64 – 88 p 82. Once again, Trent was pleased to note that as pervasive as the misunderstanding was, it hadn't managed to infect the good Dr Cupboard.

Dr Cupboard himself had often taken, according to Dr Hubert Cupboard, *Coming out of the Cupboard*, (Oxford: Oxford University Press, 1990). While he was working on Dr Hubert Cupboard, *Towards an Attitude of Rectitude* (Oxford: Oxford University Press, 1984)[21], he had often walked this route. In his autobiography he remarked that "the mindless concentration required to cross over roads and wait at road islands until the next road could be traversed was something strangely similar to the process of assimilating ethical assertions"[22]. He must have walked the route as often as Trent, if not more, during the course of writing *Towards an Attitude of Rectitude*.

Trent reached the British Library and munched on his loaf of bread a bit more. He'd probably have to get some more food on the way back home. When Dr Cupboard had been coming here, there had been a small corner shop one street down from the British Library, where he must have bought snacks and various other forms of sustenance after a hard day pawing over the tomes of research he had been reading in the British Library. From the size of the bibliography in the back of *Towards an Attitude of Rectitude*, he had done a lot of pawing.

Trent retrieved his copy of *Assessing Certitude*, removed the bookmark, and continued from where he left off. "In making this judgement there is a necessary element of ethical doubt, which cannot simply be ignored

---

21 Trent had read it for the first time in the Bodleian in Oxford. The copy he had has some graffiti in which someone had changed a "b" for a "w" in the phrase "I, of all people, would not bank on the modern world's understanding of rectitude as a theoretical principle". Trent had not found it amusing. Evidentially, though, a number of people had, and only two months later, the graffiti-er made a sequel, in changing Cupboard to Cock-head. This second piece of graffiti achieved, Trent mused, the almost impossible accomplishment of being even less witty than the original.

22 As he remembered this phrase, Trent found himself pressing the button underneath a pedestrian light, and waiting for the red man to step aside so that the green man could usher him across.

by reference to tangential application," he read. "For example, when one chooses to determine the exact non-mandatory value, assigned to any single element, one finds a non-porous barrier to further advancement[23]; the passing through of which introduces the non certitude inherent in this process".

Trent imagined Dr Cupboard sitting down at this exact table and pondering over his research. No doubt the good doctor had been chewing on the end of his pencil (pens were not allowed in the reading room in case ink was spilled on the books.) He imagined Dr Cupboard flicking through a thick yellowing tome, and excitedly jotting down: "Judgement leads to doubt – ethical? Tangential application – reference? No."

Back at his typewriter that evening, Dr Cupboard, would have collected together his notes, and pored over them.[24] Carefully, he would have begun developing his scrawled handwritten notes into the beginnings of *Towards an Attitude of Rectitude*.

Dr Cupboard would have sat there, contemplating, thinking, puzzling over his wording. "In this judgement there is"... no, start with the judgement. "This judgement introduces"... well, does it introduce it? Actually, it's not really the judgement itself, is it, it's the act of making the judgement. "In making this judgement" – yes, that's good, that's exactly the point. "In making this

---

23 Trent scratched at his ear as he read this and puzzled over it for a few minutes. "When one chooses to determine the exact non-mandatory value", "non-mandatory" must mean not compulsory, so, free choice. "Value", well, he'd probably find out exactly what sort of value Dr Cupboard meant in a minute. He carried on "assigned to any single element", so, the "value" (still wasn't sure what "value") given to a single "element". Element of what? He'd probably find that out in a few minutes as well, when he found out what sort of "value" he was talking about.

24 Trent did a similar thing with the notes he took on Dr Hubert Cupboard, typing them up neatly when he got back in the evening, and cataloguing them in a large cross indexed ring binder.

judgement there is a new doubt introduced"... well, maybe not, but he was on a roll now, he'd just carry with on with the flow. He'd come back and tidy up the odds and ends, just put the icing on the cake when he finished.

"It is not reasonable to assume that this doubt can be countered" (countered was the wrong word, but he couldn't think what the right one was for the minute. Placeholder words, like this, he found, were often very useful in letting him carry on flowing once he was on a roll. Scheeze, he hadn't been on a roll like this since... must have been chapter 2 of *Initiating Thought in a Co-existent Manner*.) "...this doubt can be countered", he continued, "by tangential application". Probably needs an example now, just to make the point crystal clear for those who haven't been paying attention. Because there would be some, he could imagine them now, in the Cambridge UL, or the Bod, sitting there, scratching their ears[25], trying to fight their way through his prose. Probably best to put an example in for their benefit. "For example", he wrote (make it clear to them that it is an example), "when I determine"... should he use the first person? Probably not, but that was a job for later. "When I determine the possible value of a single element, there is a type of barrier preventing me from advancing further." Did that make his point? It wasn't quite as elegant as he liked.

Dr Cupboard paused and returned to the beginning of the section Now that he'd got it all done, he could tidy up the corners. "In making this judgement there is a new doubt introduced. It is not reasonable to assume that this doubt can be countered..." Okay, start off at the beginning. He didn't like "new doubt". A little bit vague. Maybe it would be better to say what it was now. "There is an element of doubt." A *necessary* element of

---

25 Trent felt his ear itching again. Was his eczema back in his ear? He'd probably have to get some of that cream for it again.

doubt. And ethical doubt, in fact. "In making this judgement there is a necessary element of ethical doubt." That pretty much made his point, but, really he wanted to carry straight on. He'd had a new sentence next, but that made it seemed rather clipped. It would probably be better to stick a "which" or a "that" in and carry on. He decided on a "which". "Which cannot reasonably be countered." No, countered was wrong. Ignored? It was more right than countered. And was reasonably right as well? "Which cannot *simply* be ignored." That's better. What can it not be ignored by. Tangential application. *Reference* to tangential application. That's better. Anyway, the example now; better get rid of that first person.

Should I turn it passive? "When it is determined"... no, sounds a bit convoluted. When one determines. Ah, that's better. Or, even better, when one chooses to determine. Ah, yes. "When one chooses to determine the possible"... no, no one chooses to determine the possible value, they choose to determine the exact value. So: "When one chooses to determine the exact, non-mandatory value given"... *assigned* to a single... "any single element, one finds a barrier to further advancement." The end probably needed a bit of work on it still, but he could work on that later.

Dr Cupboard sat back and scratched his head. Probably, he decided, time for something to eat. Lunch? Dinner? It didn't really matter which one, one of them. Brunch? Supper? Breakfast? Tea? He lost track of which one was which. How late did brunch have to be before it became lunch? How small did lunch have to be before it became a snack? The terms were nebulous and inherently ambiguous. He'd have some food. There, you couldn't go wrong with that. Probably be a good analogy somewhere, he thought.

He had a look through his pantry, and found it surprisingly sparse. Strange, he thought. What he really needed was some carbohydrates, he suspected. Bread, then. Or potatoes. But potatoes probably had to be heated up or something. He crossed to his breadbin, and pulled out a lump in a brown paper bag. He must have had the same idea earlier on, he realised, although he couldn't remember doing it, for the bread was already half eaten. He shrugged, and began to finish off the loaf. Tomorrow, he decided, he'd take the day off. The reading room could wait until Thursday.

About the Contributors

Miriam Arkush is currently in her second year at Jesus College, Cambridge studying Theology. Born and bred in South Hertfordshire (which she likes to call London) Miriam's involvement with art began in school, where she was encouraged to study basic design in painting and art history.

Marina Bradbury studied Modern Languages at Jesus College from 2003 – 2007. She spent her year abroad in Paris and thinks she might like to go back there to live one day. Whilst she will be sad to leave Cambridge she is looking forward to having more time to spend on her art.

Adam Crothers was born in Belfast in 1984, and has studied at Trinity College Dublin and at Cambridge, where he won the Quiller-Couch Prize for creative writing in 2005. He is currently a graduate student at Girton College, writing a PhD thesis on rhyme in English-language poetry.

Naomi Grant studies English at Jesus College, Cambridge. She studies with the painter, Israel Zohar, in London.

Emma Hoare is an MPhil American Literature student at Jesus College, Cambridge. She graduated from Balliol College, Oxford, in 2003, and moved to Japan. She is currently writing a book set in Osaka, which is turning out to be the usual first novel exercise in personal score-settling and dreadful mid-twenties angst.

Laura Hocking is a finalist in Modern Languages at St John's, Cambridge. She has written two short plays, a score of songs and some poems, which have been published in student magazines – one of which, InPrint, she now co-edits. She plans to study screenwriting.

Meirion Jordan is a fourth-year mathematics student at Somerville College, Oxford. His work has previously appeared in Poetry Wales and the TLS, and his first collection of poetry is due to be published by Seren in 2008. He is on the longlist for an Eric Gregory award this year.

Claire Lowdon is a third year English student at New College, Oxford. She has lived in Wiltshire for most of her life.

Muireann Maguire (Jesus College, Cambridge) is midway through a PhD on supernatural themes in 20th-century Russian literature. She has spent a year learning Russian in Moscow and a year teaching English in Krasnoyarsk, central Siberia. She is originally from Dingle, Co. Kerry, Ireland. In 2001 her first poetry collection, *The Nightingale Seed*, was published by Lapwing Press.

Heather Mcrobie is studying History and Politics at Keble College, Oxford. Due to a healthily 'relaxed' attitude to academic achievements, she neglected to actually sit her Finals in 2006, so finishes this summer. She's starting a Masters in Montreal in September, before going to American law-school. Her first novel, *Psalm 119*, is being published by Maia Press in early 2008.

Eric Morgan is in his final year studying for a BA in law at University College, Oxford. He was born in Toronto, Canada and received a BA in Economics from the University of Toronto where he was the editor of the Hart House Literary Review.

Christopher Morley is a member of Keble College, Oxford, where he is studying for an M.Phil. in Landscape Archaeology. When he is not studying he works as a professional field archaeologist. His interests are writing, photography and prehistory, and he is also a fan of real ale and everything that goes with it.

Benjamin Morris is a native of Mississippi but is now a first-year PhD student in cultural heritage studies at Cambridge. Educated at Duke, Edinburgh, and Cambridge, his work has been published and won recognition in both the US and the UK, including a Pushcart nomination, the Chancellor's Medal for an English Poem (Cambridge), and a Commendation in the 2006 National Poetry Competition (UK).

Marcelle Olivier is studying for a DPhil in African Archaeology at Keble College, Oxford. She has previously completed degrees in Drama, and English Literature, and tried her hand at high school teaching before (hastily) returning to university. Originally from South Africa, Marcelle has published both poetry and short fiction in various journals and anthologies. She enjoys the work of Marina Tsvetaeva, Arthur Nortje, Ken Barris and Dorothy Parker.

Rachel Piercey (St Hugh's, Oxford) loves writing about anecdotes she hears, or strange stories she happens upon, and she loves half-rhyme and internal rhyme. She would like to thank the shadowy woman in the park, Sir Walter Raleigh for the puddle incident, and her friends at OUPS for their support and advice.

Simon Pitt is a second year student at Selwyn College, Cambridge. Despite a lack of visible evidence he is in the middle of studying an English degree. His hobbies include going to the theatre, eating doughnuts and making judgements about people based solely on their choice of hat.

Beatrice Priest is the Levy-Plumb Student Artist-in-Residence at Christ's College, Cambridge. She graduated in 2006 from Emmanuel with a degree in French and Spanish. While she has most extensively painted the female body, she is interested in diverse material, ranging from medieval French literature to the Utah desert. She is holding her end of year exhibition at Christ's this May Week.

David Ranc is reading for a PhD in International Studies at Trinity Hall Cambridge and researches 'Identification, Football & the Press in Europe after the Bosman ruling 1995'. He has also published as a photographer and teaches photography in the summer.

Ryan Roark grew up in Texas and graduated in 2005 from Brown University with degrees in maths, biology, and comparative literature. She is currently in the second year of a PhD in oncology at St. John's College, Cambridge. She spends most of her free time writing or editing student publications, including the *Mays*, *BlueSci*, and *The Cambridge Student*.

Neil Singh is a 4th year Medical Student at Trinity Hall, Cambridge. Writing both poetry and song lyrics, Neil has read alongside Simon Armitage, John Agard and Carol Ann Duffy, and been tutored by Hugo Williams. His poems have been published by *Forward Press* and in *Contraband* and *Filament*. He is currently writing a collection of poetry on the theme of health and disease.

Francesca Whitlum-Cooper is a first year English student at Emmanuel College, Cambridge. She is an active member of the university's drama scene, having directed her own production of Mamet's "Sexual Perversity in Chicago" in February, and performed in three productions this year. "Last Words" will be her first published story.

Typeset in Linotype Didot 12 on 14 by Ryan Roark
on a lay-out designed by David Ranc

Produced by LPPS Ltd in Malta

Submissions were accepted from any matriculated member of the Universities of Oxford and Cambridge, up to one year after their graduation. This year four hundred students submitted seven hundred poems, two hundred short stories and novel extracts, and two hundred items of visual art. Each piece was read by at least three members of a committee of current Cambridge students. The resulting longlists of poetry and prose were sent to the guest editors, Sean O'Brien and Colm Tóibín respectively, who made and introduced the final selections. The entire process was anonymous.